Who's Afraid of the Working Class?

trash
ANDREW BOVELL

money
PATRICIA CORNELIUS

dream-town
MELISSA REEVES

suit
CHRISTOS TSIOLKAS

requiem
(musical score)
IRINE VELA

edited by Julian Meyrick

CURRENCY PLAYS
First published 2000
Currency Press Ltd,
PO Box 2287, Strawberry Hills, NSW, 2012, Australia
enquiries@currency.com.au
www.currency.com.au

in *Melbourne Stories*.

This edition first published in 2014.

Reprinted 2017.

Introduction © Julian Meyrick 2000, 2014; *Who's Afraid of the Working Class?* © Andrew
Bovell, Patricia Cornelius, Melissa Reeves, Christos Tsiolkas, Irine Vela, 2000, 2014

Cataloguing-in-publication data for this title is available from the National Libary Website:
www.nla.gov.au

Typeset by Emily Ralph and Paul O'Beirne for Currency Press.
Cover design by Katy Wall for Currency Press.
Front cover shows Bruce Morgan as Kennett Boy in the 1998 Melbourne Workers Theatre
production. (Photo: Viv Méhes)

Contents

Currency Press acknowledges the Traditional Owners of the Country on which we live and work. We pay our respects to all Aboriginal and Torres Strait Islander Elders, past and present.

ANDREW BOVELL has received numerous awards for his work in stage, film, television and radio. His stage credits include *Speaking in Tongues, Distant Lights From Dark Places, Scenes From A Separation* (co-written with Hannie Rayson), *Ship of Fools, After Dinner* and *The Ballad of Lois Ryan*.

PATRICIA CORNELIUS is a founding member of Melbourne Workers Theatre. Her plays include *Lilly and May, Jack's Daughters, Max, The Aftermath, Taxi, No Fear, Last Drinks, Opa—A Sexual Odyssey, Home of a Stranger, Platform, Hogs Hairs* and *Leeches*. Patricia also works as a director and dramaturg.

JULIAN MEYRICK is a freelance director. His previous work includes *Grace Among the Christians, St Rose of Lima, Fun and Games with the Oresteia,* all by Luke Devenish; Garcia Lorca's *The Love of Don Perlimplin;* Reinhardt Goering's *Dreadnought;* Douglas Stewart's *Ned Kelly* (adapted by Pam Leversha); *Barry Collins Judgement* and *Quarter Hour Stories* for Melbourne University. In 1998 he received the Victorian Green Room Award for Best Director on the Fringe.

MELISSA REEVES is a Melbourne playwright. Her plays include *In Cahoots, The Girl I Love* (co-written with Margaret Mills, Maude Davey and Nicki Redlich), *Sweettown* (awarded the Jill Blewitt Playwrights Award in 1993), *Great Day, The Emperor's New Clothes, The Sign of the Phantom, Storming Heaven* and *Road Movie*.

CHRISTOS TSIOLKAS is the author of the novels *Loaded* (filmed as *Head On* by Ana Kokkinos) and *The Jesus Man* and has published with collaborator Sasha Soldatow the dialogue *Jump Cuts*. He directed the short film *Thug* with Spiro Economopolous. His plays include *Viewing Blue Poles* and a contemporary adaptation of the Electra myth.

IRINE VELA has worked as a composer on dozens of music theatre productions with companies such as the Melbourne Workers Theatre, Playbox, Canto Coro, IRAA, Arena, the Victorian College of the Arts, Deckchair Theatre and Circus Oz. Some of her credits include *The Ballad of Lois Ryan, Opa—A Sexual Odyssey, Black Cargo* and *Kate 'N' Shiner*. She is a founding member of the Greek-Australian music group the haBiBis.

INTRODUCTION

So seamless was the evolution and production of *Who's Afraid of the Working Class?* that it is impossible to separate out individual achievements from the impact of the show as a whole. Born from anger, tempered by craft, it is also hard to believe that such a significant piece of work could be *fun* to produce. Yet it was. The lead in this, as in the form and content of the show, came from the writers. For me the conventional image of the playwright as the person at the back of the auditorium squirming in pain as 'their' play is murdered in performance, was buried forever by the patience, skill and flexibility of the four writers and composer who together made up the *Who's Afraid...?* creative team. It was the creative team who advised my employment as director; who set deadlines for drafts and gave advice on re-writing, cuts and scene order; who assisted through an excruciating casting process; who understood when things went wrong, applauded when things went right, and provided practical help when things hung in the balance. Working with such a group is like riding a rocket: you go where it is fired, hanging on as best you can. Once or twice you kick your ankles and steer a bit. But right from the start you know that an extraordinary creative unfolding is taking place and the job of the production process is to give it the fullest possible stage expression.

The script reproduced here marks the end of what in effect was a three-year development period. During this time many forces came together to realise the original scripts and in turn to influence them. Not the least of these were the cast themselves who, comprising only six actors, had to portray nineteen different characters in eighteen separate scenes. The first months were spent in researching the project and agreeing core values. By the time I came on board these had been settled and the significance of the creative team's artistic and political direction was apparent. It flowed from one key experience. Early in 1997 the writers and composer went to a pub in West Melbourne famous for its vibrant, resistive, blue-collar atmosphere. What they found was a commercial shell, rattling with cable TV and pokies. In its hollowness and venality it seemed to sum up the vast betrayal the Kennett Government had perpetrated on all Victorians. Here indeed was an answer to the question the writers had been briefed with: who was afraid of the working class—*no-one*.

The choice of the aesthetic entailed considerable risk. It meant breaking with the upbeat, celebrational mood of so much Australian community theatre, a style with which the commissioning company, the Melbourne Workers

Theatre, was partially identified. There was always the fear of being negative, regressive even, painting things as worse than they were. But how could they be any worse than what we saw, daily, around us? As rehearsals for the first season got underway it was easy to research the characters in the play. All you had to do was walk down the street. The most frightening thing was that the notion of poverty itself had changed. What was once simple deprivation is now hedged about by the torments of a hundred concocted consumer needs. Not to be able to afford a certain style of clothes, or car, or level of service, is to spiral down into a social void where traditional notions of class and consciousness give way to a broader experience of loss and devastation. Australia has indeed become a more 'open' and 'flexible' society. Now anyone has the right to be marginalised.

Trashed, crushed, frustrated, full of hate and pain, the men and women of *Who's Afraid...?* are demonstrably *not* working—or working, at best, in the dark pockets of an urban world. Only six of the characters we meet are employed, and of these two are prostitutes and two police. They are not potential revolutionaries waiting for a Great Red Dawn to sweep the way to a better world order. They are, if not 'ordinary' people, then certainly average. They focus on themselves because the pressures under which they labour are so unremitting they have little energy for anything else. Sometimes this is expressed in behaviour towards others that is angry, cruel or self-destructive. Sometimes despite outward circumstances, generosity, kindness and sympathy assert themselves. But it is always touch and go. These are lives balanced on a knife edge. A great deal of rehearsal was spent trying to understand the emotional complexities of compromised lives and feeding the results into the structure of the production. As in all important theatre experiences, the journey was both an inward and an outward one. The more we struggled to realise the play, the more we were forced to look around at the world we imagined we were speaking about.

There were many conversations about who these characters represented. New-style underclass or old-style lumpen proletariate? As the latter did they deserve our sympathy since they were—without exception—entirely lacking in traditional notions of class consciousness? Indeed, they hardly seemed to be political at all. It is highly unlikely that any of them would do anything as positive as join a union picket line. Instead, they present an entirely different side of political oppression: its cost. These are men and women who struggle not politically, heroically, resistively, but baldly, personally, in anguish. They struggle not to overcome but simply to stay alive. If they had a choice perhaps they wouldn't be political at all. But they don't have a choice. They have had, as it were, politics thrust upon them. Or rather, they have had visited on their ordinary but nevertheless coherent lives, the costs of an economic and political system which doesn't seem to care anymore how many families it wrecks, lives it smashes or careers it destroys as long as it can achieve its increasingly abstract goals.

The play opened on 1 May 1997 at Trades Hall, smack in the middle of the MUA wharf dispute. The building was alive with the comings and goings of officials and pickets, with news about Patrick Stevedores, workers' rights, employers' duties and political resistance. It was a galvanising moment for many people, including some who until then had thought of themselves as non-political. The play, with its message of structurally-induced personal pain, appeared in the right place at the right time. For any show to touch a nerve it needs more than the skills of the artists producing it, however talented. It needs the sympathy and understanding of its intended spectators and it is hard to say at the end of the day which was the more amazing: the fact that *Who's Afraid...?* was produced in the way that it was, or that Melbourne audiences heard it.

The form of the plays is 'cool' and realistic. This was the choice of the writers and it suits the subject matter. The ultimate goal, simply stated, was to put stories on stage which would not otherwise be heard. Theatre can do this. In the current passion for mixed-media and performance-style events, it can be forgotten that theatre, a public medium, operates not only visually and physically but intellectually, as a vehicle for ideas. With courage and skill these ideas can make a leading contribution to contemporary debates. The challenge this presents theatre artists is not only one of style but one of truth. How to say what must be said yet stay true to the experience of putting it on stage? In this respect, the audacity, even savagery of the writing, deserves comment. The late critic Harry Kippax once called theatre the home of old ideas. And so it often seems when show after show paraphrases what has been said earlier and to greater effect by television and film. Over the years and without much of a struggle, theatre has gone onto the back foot, more afraid of what it stands to lose by tackling accepted stereotypes than what it has to gain by broaching fresh perceptions. As a result, it has often compromised its immediacy, lucidity and emotional force.

This is not the case with *Who's Afraid...?*. Grappling with the dark underbelly of contemporary urban living, the writing pulls no punches in showing the resulting conflict. This is not a desire to shock for its own sake. It is a considered choice, one which saw everyone involved in the development of the project examine their consciences before committing themselves to material whose reception might well be very negative (and on occasions was). The costs of representing threshold material are high, both for artists and audience. In the words of Augusto Boal: 'the image of the real is real in so far as it is an image'. The courage of the writers had to be matched by the courage of everyone involved with the production, and it is to the credit of the actors especially that they so willingly engaged with the frequently painful task of portraying complex and troubled behaviour on stage.

Once *Who's Afraid...?* started touring conventional theatres for audiences who did not share the frame of local awareness of their Melbourne counterparts, the meaning of the show changed. From being a play for Victoria it became a play about Victoria. From being a cry of anger it became a cry of warning. Though the form of the show remained the same, the thinking behind it was reshaped. The creative team used to say that if a play is political then it must be *better* in every way than a non-political one or else it will simply be dismissed as propaganda. Likewise, the production had to work hard to seamlessly adapt to the different physical circumstances and expectations of mainstream theatre. Again history came to the rescue. 1999 was not 1997. By now serious doubts about the political and economic agenda of the New Right were making themselves heard all over the country. Once again, the show found itself in and of its time.

Born from Jeff Kennett's Victoria, it was fitting that the first production of *Who's Afraid...?* ended at the same time as the political regime which it so trenchantly criticised. If the popular reaction to the show was a surprise, who could have guessed that a government tipped for another eight years in office could be so unceremoniously cast aside? It is too much to hope that any theatre can ever be directly responsible for such a reaction. But if it helps focus thoughts and feelings marginalised by the major media, then the place of the art form in society at large is now more important than ever.

The *Who's Afraid...?* project aimed to serve its immediate community at the highest level of skill and imagination. If it represents anything it is less a perfect product than a perfect process. It was the outcome of a team of dedicated theatre professionals who proved beyond all doubt that achievement in the theatre is *always* the result of collaboration. The scripts were part of a living whole, the DNA structure by which the body of the production was brought into existence. This is how they should be read now: not as words on a page, but as voices in the head; as an indication, an invitation, a resolution, a world waiting to happen.

Julian Meyrick
Director and editor
Melbourne Workers Theatre production

Who's Afraid of the Working Class was first produced by Melbourne Workers Theatre at the Victorian Trades Hall, Melbourne, on 1 May 1998 with the following cast:

O'MANNEY, COP 2, LEON, MAN IN BED	David Adamson
MAN, JAMES	Glenn Shea
STACEY, TRISHA	Daniela Farinacci
RHONDA, WOMAN IN BED, PROSTITUTE, GINA, COP 1	Eugenia Fragos
DANIEL, ORTON, YOUNG BOY	Bruce Morgan
WOMAN, TRAIN GIRL, KATINA	Maria Theodorakis

Musicians: David Abiuso (bass) and Helen Mountford (cello)

Director, Julian Meyrick
Composer, Irine Vela
Assistant Director, Jude Sears
Designer, Greg Clarke
Lighting Designer, Paul Jackson
Production Manager, Chris Harris
Stage Manager, Meg White

CHARACTERS

SUIT

BOY
JAMIE
CLAIRE
MR O'MANNEY
GINA

MONEY

MAN
WOMAN
DANIEL
GIRL
MAN
MUSICIAN
OLD WOMAN

DREAM-TOWN

KATINA
TRISHA
LEON
COP
COP TWO

TRASH

ORTON
STACEY
JAMIE
RHONDA

The program was originally presented by an ensemble of six actors.

SUIT

KENNETT BOY MONOLOGUE

A YOUNG BOY *in his mid-teens comes onto the stage.*

I love Jeff Kennett. I think he's a good guy, a sexy guy. I like it that he's tall, I like it that he's smart, I like it that he doesn't give a shit about anyone. He's an arsehole, I know that. He's a cunt. It's obvious. He's a silver-spoon-up-his-arse cunt, he can't hide that, but I don't care. He's not whingeing all the time, not bludging, not making excuses. He's got style; he looks good and he knows it; he's got class. It's written all over him. But, he's not soft. He's not soft at all.

Not like my dad. No, not at all like my dad. My old man is one of those guys who's wasted his whole fucking life. He works a shit job, has for thirty fucking years, since he was a kid, pouring concrete. And, man, you should listen to him, listen to him go on about it. 'I'm so tough, we brickies are so special.' Yeah, right. Hasn't done a fucking thing with his life. Hasn't seen the world, hasn't had an original thought. Nothing tough about him except his mouth and his forearms and even they're going to fat. My mum's no different. She's brain-dead as well.

My father hates Jeff Kennett, calls him scum, says he's destroying the unions and the working class. But I can tell that deep down inside he respects him. You've gotta. Kennett doesn't give a shit about anyone, does whatever he likes. He even stands up to that ugly piece of shit, Howard. And that's the leader of his fucking party! Kennett is a legend. Bet my old man wouldn't mind being like that, instead of following orders all his fucking life. Weak cunt! Just a day, just one day, I'd like to see my father be like Kennett. Just fucking once.

I want to go down on Kennett. When I do go down on a guy, when I come to that, it'll *have* to be someone like him. Tough. Arrogant. Knows what he wants. That's my favourite wank dream. I'm with school, an excursion to Parliament House. Somehow—I skip over this bit while I'm pulling off—Kennett and I end up in a lift. It's him and it's me. Sometimes there's this other guy, some suited, young, wog guy I saw on the Channel Nine News, some wog guy who hangs around Kennett. Sometimes he's there, banging away with us, sometimes he just watches. And then sometimes he's not there at all.

The lift stops. There's a moment that the light flicks off, then it flickers back on again. Kennett puts a hand on my shoulder. He's way tall, way taller than me. He notices I've got a stiffie in my school pants, I'm stretching the cotton. He's dressed real fine. Beautiful suit, slim tie. He winks at me and then it's on.

Every time I wank to this, it changes. Sometimes he's hairy, blonde curls, all over his chest and stomach. Sometimes he's smooth. He doesn't take off his clothes, just opens his shirt, unzips the pants. I dream that his dick is squat and thick, and that when he comes, he comes in fucking buckets. Just pours the come over me, over the wog guy. That's my favourite wank.

Fuck! I could come now. Man, I could come all over this fucking stage.

I wish I could tell my father about this dream. Maybe that would get the cunt alive. Poofter son, father, you've got a poofter son who wants to fuck a real bloke like Kennett, not some boring working stiff like you. He'd crack, I know he'd crack it. How to tell his mates on the job? 'My son's a faggott.' Gutless cunt. He could never do that.

Kennett, when he got elected, there was this big rally in the city. It was fucking enormous, about a hundred and fifty thousand people. He had closed down my old high school, that fucking waste of space. It was nothing but a factory churning out dole casualties. They should've torched the place long ago. But Mum and Dad, of course, Mum and Dad were angry. [*Mimicking*] 'You got to come to the rally, it's important.'

So I had to go, with Mum and Dad. Dad kept bumping into all his scuzzy alco mates; even the young ones looked sick from their shitty useless jobs. I liked the crowd, it was exciting, I loved being there in all that mass. I thought we could do anything, fucking pull apart this shithole of a city if we wanted. I wanted it to get angrier, I wanted it to get bloody, like it happens on the news overseas. The cops were there, waiting. I wanted it to get bloody, so I could bash some cunt cop right in the middle of his fat, ugly face. I wanted to kill a cop, then go right off and torch fucking Chinatown. That would have been a fucking winner, man. Kill a cop and kill a gook. But it wasn't that kind of rally. It was [*contemptuously, in an effeminate accent*] political.

I managed to get up close, near Parliament steps, next to this really drugged-out feral chick and her dread-head, dead-head mates. I sat near the steps, bored now that the marching had stopped. Some union wanker was going on, whingeing about what everybody already knew. 'The government doesn't care about hospitals, Kennett doesn't care about education. This government sucks.' [*Shouting*] All governments suck, you brain-dead cunt!

I looked up. In the window there was Kennett, looking down. Some ponsey guys around him were nervous, shitting their pants because of the crowd. But not Kennett. Nah, not Kennett. You know what he was doing, you know what the cunt was doing? Kennett was laughing. He was watching us and he was laughing at us.

That moment, that's the moment I knew he was a God. That's the moment I thought you are one smart mother-fucker. All around me people were singing union songs. Crap hippie shit. We shall bloody overcome for Christsakes. I looked around, looked around, saw my old man. There he was, little Sammy Destanzo, little Sammy who hasn't done one thing of any note in his whole wasted fucking life. Little Sammy Destanzo who is forty-six and fucking looks sixty-eight. There's my old man, chanting along, doing the old nazi salute to Kennett who doesn't know who the fuck Sammy Destanzo is and who will never know who Sammy Destanzo is because Sammy Destanzo is a big, fat nothing.

I couldn't wait to leave this crowd of morons, these fucking sheep.

Dad says to me, do you want a job on a building site, and I just look at him. A real dirty look. He goes ape-shit, calls me a bludging cunt. I don't listen. He wants me to work on a building site, he wants me to be like him. I'd rather sell my body for twenty bucks in St Kilda, I'd rather be a fucking whore. Work, grog, sleep. Work, grog, sleep. Work, grog, sleep.

That's it, that's my old man. Three lousy little words.

I'd like to fuck Kennett. That would be the best. I reckon he's got a hairy arse and big red balls. I'd like to fucking ram it right up him. I'd like to do it again and again. That would be cunt worth fucking.

One day I'm out of here. I'm not going to be trapped in fucking Dandenong watching that dumb, plastic arsehole Ray Martin night after night. One day I'm going to have lots of money. I'll steal it, I'll beg for it. Fuck, to get out of here, I'd kill for it. I'll get style, I'll learn about the coolest places to be, I'll have all the best-looking guys hanging on me, begging to have a go at sucking my dick.

One day I'll be above Jeff Kennett. I'll be above all of you, you'll all be little specks, little nine-to-five, seven-to-three-thirty little earthworms.

Work. Till you drop.

Drink beer. Till you rot.

Sleep. That's the best part of your lives.

He spits on the stage.

I can't wait to vote.

He exits.

❖ ❖ ❖ ❖ ❖

MONEY

SCENE ONE: MONEY

Three figures, a MAN, *a* WOMAN *and an adolescent boy,* DANIEL. *The* MAN *and* WOMAN *stand together, but apart. They are quietly agitated.* DANIEL *stands alone.*

MAN: Ask someone, just a loan, just for a while, we'll pay it back as soon as we can.

WOMAN: Who?

MAN: Ask your mother.

WOMAN: I've asked her. We didn't pay her back the last time.

MAN: Ask your sister.

WOMAN: She asked us.

MAN: Ask your friend with the money.

WOMAN: We've lost touch.

MAN: Ask your uncle.

WOMAN: He's got none.

MAN: Ask Mrs Sands.

WOMAN: She's as skint as we are. You ask.

MAN: Who?

WOMAN: Try the bank.

MAN: And let them know we've got none.

WOMAN: Ask your mother.

MAN: I've asked her. We didn't pay her back the last time.

WOMAN: Ask a friend.

MAN: They've got none.

WOMAN: Ask anyone.

BOTH: What about…? No. What about…? No. There's no one.

> *Silence.*

MAN: I know what you're thinking.

WOMAN: You're wrong, I'm not.

MAN: You think about it all the time.

WOMAN: I don't.

MAN: I'm trying.

WOMAN: I know you are.

MAN: I don't like it any more than you do.

WOMAN: I know that.

MAN: Then get off my back for a while.

WOMAN: Who's blaming you?

MAN: You are.

WOMAN: You couldn't help it.

MAN: I couldn't.

WOMAN: It was bad luck.

MAN: See, see what I mean?

WOMAN: What?

MAN: Luck had nothing to do with it.

WOMAN: All I meant was—

MAN: You meant it was me, it was my lack of judgement—

WOMAN: I didn't.

   Pause.

MAN: There's an easy way out, you know.

WOMAN: Here we go.

MAN: Sell it.

WOMAN: Here we go.

MAN: It's a load of crap.

WOMAN: I don't think so.

MAN: It will solve the problem.

WOMAN: No it won't.

MAN: Of course it will. Every month it's the same. If we dump the place we don't have to face it. Every month! Every bloody month.

WOMAN: And then what?

MAN: What?

WOMAN: And then what? Pay rent, that's what. Every month. Every bloody month.

MAN: It'll be cheaper.

WOMAN: No it won't and it won't be mine.

MAN: We'll get something smaller.

   DANIEL *looks at them for a moment.*

WOMAN: What do you mean smaller? How can we go smaller? [*Pause.*] I'm on to you.

MAN: A flat. We'll get a flat.

WOMAN: We've got a house.

MAN: We can't afford it.

WOMAN: What's it got to do with you?

MAN: What do you mean by that?

WOMAN: It's not your problem. I find it. I always do.

MAN: You find it?

WOMAN: Yes I do.

MAN: I'm not contributing anything, I suppose.

WOMAN: No, not much.

MAN: Bullshit.

WOMAN: Not much.

MAN: I own half of it, you know. [*Pause*.] I'm just telling you, it's half mine.

WOMAN: This house is mine.

MAN: Half yours.

WOMAN: All mine.

MAN: Not by law.

WOMAN: I pay the payments on this house. Always have done.

MAN: All I'm saying is that by law this house is half mine.

WOMAN: You don't give a damn about this house. I wanted it, it was my deposit, I pay the mortgage, it's mine.

MAN: If I left I'd get half this house. By law. I'd get half.

WOMAN: Well, we're stuck with each other then.

MAN: Is that what we are?

WOMAN: What?

MAN: Stuck? Stuck with one another?

WOMAN: Yes, that's what we are.

MAN: Is that all we are?

WOMAN: Yes, yes that's about it.

MAN: That's it?

WOMAN: Yes, yes, that's it… Oh, I don't know. I think so.

MAN: You never touch me anymore.

WOMAN: [*astounded*] You never touch me! You haven't touched me for years.

MAN: You don't want me to touch you.

WOMAN: You don't want to touch me.

MAN: I do.

WOMAN: Since when?

MAN: I want to touch you now.

WOMAN: How come?

MAN: I don't know. I just do.

WOMAN: Come on then, touch me.

MAN: Now?

WOMAN: You said you wanted to, come on, touch me then.

> *They come together tentatively and kiss. The kiss is tender but lifeless and they part.*

MAN: If I did leave, I'd get half, that's all I'm saying.

WOMAN: There is no way you're going to get my house, not half of it, not any of it, so forget it.

Silence. The MAN *puts on his suit coat.*

When are you going to stop this? It's ridiculous.

MAN: Something will come up and no one will be the wiser.

WOMAN: Why don't you tell him? He's eighteen. He can handle it.

MAN: I don't want him to know.

WOMAN: Why not? What's the big deal?

MAN: I don't want him to know.

WOMAN: He probably knows.

MAN: Only if you told him.

WOMAN: I didn't tell him.

MAN: I don't want him to know.

WOMAN: He's not stupid. He can work it out. He knows there's no money.

DANIEL *stands between them.*

DANIEL: I need some money.

MAN: [*together*] Ha! Ask your mother.

WOMAN: [*together*] Ha! Ask your father.

DANIEL: I need some money.

WOMAN: There's none.

DANIEL: I need some.

MAN: What for?

DANIEL: For fares.

WOMAN: Where you going?

MAN: Nowhere.

DANIEL: For food.

MAN: Eat here.

DANIEL: I want to go out.

MAN: Take a sandwich.

DANIEL: I want to visit some friends.

MAN: Don't need money for that.

DANIEL: I want to go to the pictures.

MAN: Watch TV.

DANIEL: I need some money.

MAN: There is none.

DANIEL: Give me an allowance.

MAN: Give you nothing.

DANIEL: How am I expected to live?

MAN: Can't help you there.

DANIEL: I need some money.

MAN: Don't ask. Don't ask anymore, there is none. You want money, go find some. There's none here to give you. Go somewhere else and ask.

DANIEL: Where?

MAN: I don't know. Go out there. Find out for yourself.

DANIEL: I've been out there. There's nothing out there.

MAN: You didn't look.

DANIEL: I looked.

MAN: Didn't look hard enough.

DANIEL: I did.

MAN: Couldn't have.

DANIEL: Why?

MAN: You would have found something.

DANIEL: There's nothing to find.

> *Frustrated, the* WOMAN *suddenly exits and returns with her purse. It's empty.*

WOMAN: My purse is empty. My purse is empty. Who took the money from my purse?

MAN: I thought you had none.

WOMAN: I had some.

MAN: I thought you had none.

WOMAN: I had some.

MAN: How come?

WOMAN: I had some put away.

MAN: Since when?

WOMAN: I borrowed some.

MAN: From whom?

WOMAN: From—

MAN: Bullshit.

WOMAN: What's it matter? It was for the mortgage.

MAN: For the mortgage!

WOMAN: Yes, for the mortgage.

MAN: You had seven hundred dollars?

WOMAN: Yes! Yes I just told you, I had the money for the mortgage.

MAN: Where did it come from?

WOMAN: I got it. I got it from—

MAN: Bullshit.

WOMAN: They called me in, I worked a couple of hours last week.

MAN: They haven't called you in for months. There's been no work, you told me that.

WOMAN: I don't know, it was months ago then. I've lost track. I just got paid, that's it.

MAN: Bullshit! Where did it come from? Where did you get money like that?

WOMAN: It's got nothing to do with you.

MAN: What are you doing to get money like that?

WOMAN: What do you think I'm doing?

MAN: You're doing something for that money. I don't want to know. I don't want to know anything about it.

WOMAN: It was mine and it's missing and I want to know who took it. Did you take it?

MAN: I didn't touch your money, your miracle money, your money that appears and disappears. Ask your son.

DANIEL: I didn't take your money. I didn't take it. I was just asking for some. Why would I ask if I had some?

MAN: You've done it before, Daniel.

DANIEL: I didn't take it.

WOMAN: You've done it before, Daniel.

DANIEL: But not this time, not this time I didn't. I didn't!

WOMAN: Someone took my money and I want it back.

DANIEL: Not me, Mum, not me, believe me. I know I've taken it before but not this time, not this time. I didn't do it.

WOMAN: You have done it before.

DANIEL: I didn't take it. Not this time. I didn't take your fucking money.

WOMAN: You were in my room.

MAN: What were you doing in our room?

DANIEL: When? I didn't. I didn't go into your room.

WOMAN: Don't shit me! You did go into my room. I fucking well saw you coming out.

DANIEL: I was nicking some fags. I forgot. I was just getting a couple of fags, that's all.

WOMAN: There were no fags. I ran out last night. Give me my money. Give me my money.

DANIEL: I know. The packet was empty. I didn't take your money. I didn't take it, I swear. I didn't take it!

DANIEL *leaves in a fury.*

❖ ❖ ❖ ❖

SUIT

SCENE ONE

JAMIE, *a young, attractive and stylish Aboriginal man, is lying back on a bed, fully dressed in tie and suit. He's in a cheap, rural motel room, pretty pictures of Australian flora on the walls. The radio is on the news. A porn mag is on the bed.*

NEWSREADER: Five o'clock and this is the news on 3TT-FM. Hello, this is Kerry Spencer. Negotiations between the Teachers' Unions and the Government have broken down again. At a press conference this afternoon the Minister for Education, Mr Phil Honeywell, said that officials from the Victorian Union of Teachers had been belligerent in the discussions. He claimed that their willingness to put in jeopardy the education of their students was indicative of a Union leadership who refused to accept the changing industrial landscape of the twenty-first century.

An unidentified body has been discovered in a charity clothing bin at a service station in Dandenong. As yet police investigating the discovery have not released any comments about the victim or the circumstances of their death. Listen to National Nine News at six o'clock for details as they come to hand. In Queensland, Premier Borbridge has called for a referendum on Native Title Legislation, echoing calls by the Western Australian Premier earlier this week. He said, 'Most Australians are sick of the dragging out of the negotiations to do with the High Court decision on Wik and most Australians want to see an end to the uncertainty. This is not a land rights issue but an issue of equal say and equal rights for all Australians.' The Prime Minister's office have released no statement on the Queensland Premier's comments.

A mobile phone rings. JAMIE *springs to it.*

JAMIE: Yes. Jamie Parker here. [*Pause.*] No, I haven't. Sorry.

He returns to lying on the bed. He lights a cigarette. The mobile phone rings.

Yes. Parker here. [*Pause.*] Saturday? I guess I can. [*Pause.*] I'll get cracking immediately.

The mobile phone rings.

Parker here. [*Pause.*] No. Should I've done it? [*Pause.*] I guess so, no one told me. [*Pause.*] Yep, sorry. I understand, it won't happen again.

He puts the phone down and stubs out the cigarette. The mobile phone rings. He lets it ring till it stops. He jumps out of the bed and looks at himself in the 'mirror' (i.e. he faces the audience). There is a knock on the door. JAMIE *is still. Another knock. He doesn't move. A final knock. The mobile phone rings. He picks it up and sits on the bed.*

Hello. [*Pause.*] Yes, that's fine. She's a friend.

JAMIE *goes to the front of the stage. He plays with his tie and slicks back his hair, looking into the mirror. There is a knock on the door.*

Come in!

CLAIRE *enters. She is dressed in a red top and black skirt. She is beautiful but make-up cannot hide the fact she is no longer young.*

Sit!

CLAIRE *walks over to the bed and picks up the porno mag. She drops it, turns away, walks towards the audience and takes out a cigarette.*

[*Not looking at her*] No smoking.

CLAIRE: Sorry.

JAMIE: I hate fucking smokers. The filth you put in your bodies.

CLAIRE: Everyone's got one vice.

JAMIE: That's weakness. [*He looks at her for the first time.*] You're old.

CLAIRE: What would you like?

JAMIE: I said you're old. The agency promised me someone young.

CLAIRE: It's all right. I promise you won't be disappointed.

JAMIE: I already am.

CLAIRE: What do you like?

JAMIE: Money.

CLAIRE: What do you like to do?

JAMIE *pulls out two hundred dollars from his pocket. He throws the bills on the floor.* CLAIRE *hesitates then bends over and picks them up.* JAMIE *sticks his hand up under her skirt.*

JAMIE: I want to fuck you up the arse.

CLAIRE: I don't do that.

JAMIE: That's what the extra fifty is for.

CLAIRE: I don't do that.

JAMIE: [*turning back to her*] You're a whore, aren't you? You'll do it. [*He takes out another fifty and throws it on the floor.*] Here, now will you do it?

CLAIRE *hesitates again, then picks up the fifty.*

Whore.

CLAIRE: Yes.

JAMIE: Slut.

CLAIRE: Yes, sir.

JAMIE: Cunt.

CLAIRE: Yes, more.

> JAMIE *lies down on the bed.*

JAMIE: Strip.

> CLAIRE *starts taking off her clothes.*

Slowly, you. I've paid for an hour, right? My time, understand? My money, my time.

> CLAIRE *continues stripping.*

[*Groaning*] You are an old whore, aren't you? How long you been doing this?

CLAIRE: I told you, you won't be disappointed.

JAMIE: You clean?

CLAIRE: I'm clean.

JAMIE: You better wash, white cunt smells, you know? You know that? You know what white cunt smells of?

CLAIRE: Whatever you say, Sugar.

JAMIE: It smells like death.

> *He grabs her and sniffs her crotch.*

Yeah, you smell of it. You stink of it.

CLAIRE: [*laughing*] What can I do for you?

JAMIE: Nothing.

CLAIRE: Nothing?

> JAMIE *touches her belly.*

JAMIE: [*groaning*] Stretch marks. You are one ugly white whore, aren't you? How long you been doing this?

CLAIRE: I told you, you won't be disappointed.

JAMIE: [*rubbing his crotch*] How many guys have been up you, hey? How many guys? A thousand? Two thousand? You diseased? You're diseased all right. [*He sits up in bed.*] You washed?

CLAIRE: I'm clean.

JAMIE: You better wash, I know how white cunt smells, how white skin smells. You know how white skin smells, do you know?

CLAIRE: It smells like death.

> JAMIE *sniffs her skin, then turns away.*

JAMIE: Yeah, you smell of it.

CLAIRE: What do you like?

JAMIE: Money.

CLAIRE: [*laughing*] Isn't there anything else?

JAMIE: No.

CLAIRE: Nothing?

JAMIE: How old is your kid?

CLAIRE: I don't have a kid.

JAMIE: [*touching her belly*] Yes you do. [*Looking up at her*] Did you give it away? Is that what you did?

CLAIRE: No.

JAMIE: For money?

CLAIRE: Fuck off.

JAMIE: Was it a girl?

CLAIRE: Stop.

JAMIE: Do you think she's on the game?

CLAIRE: Stop.

JAMIE: Do you think she's whoring?

CLAIRE: I'm not listening to this.

She starts putting on her clothes. JAMIE *takes another fifty from his pocket and waves it in her face.* CLAIRE *hesitates.*

JAMIE: That's a good girl.

CLAIRE: [*her voice gentle*] Listen, mate. I don't know what your problem is. I'm here, we could have some fun. I'm not racist, I promise you. I've got heaps of Koori friends. I like you people.

JAMIE: [*interrupting*] I hate you people! You know boongs, do you, you know black whores, do you? You know black junkies, do you? Black scum, do you? They're not my people. Do you understand? They're *your* people. Got it?

CLAIRE: [*sullenly*] I got it. [*Her voices goes gentle.*] Listen, mate. We can fuck, we can do anything you like, Sugar. But I won't do this. Sorry, I can't do this. Why don't we just make love, Sugar. How about that? Why don't we just fuck, without words, I can be anyone you like. Let's just fuck.

She starts to undo JAMIE*'s tie, then undo his shirt. He springs away from her.*

JAMIE: [*shouting*] No!

He walks over to the audience. He does up his tie and his shirt. He does not look at CLAIRE.

What are you?

CLAIRE: A woman.

JAMIE: And what's your daughter?

CLAIRE: I don't have a daughter.

JAMIE: And what's your son?

CLAIRE: I don't have a son.

JAMIE: And what's your daughter?

CLAIRE: She's fifteen. She's a good kid, a nice kid.

JAMIE: And what's your daughter?

> CLAIRE *is silent.*

A white cunt. And she smells like?

CLAIRE: Please, can't we just fuck, mate? Whatever you like, fuck me up the arse. Just shut it.

JAMIE: [*turning to* CLAIRE] And she smells like?

> CLAIRE *turns away.*

And she smells like?

CLAIRE: Stop.

JAMIE: And she smells like? Come on, you know, what does she smell like, what she smell of?

CLAIRE: Enough!

JAMIE: You can't order me about. Who do you think you are? Do you know what you are? Do you? [*Shouting*] What are you?

> CLAIRE *and* JAMIE *look straight at each other and they speak at the same time:*

CLAIRE: [*together*] A woman.

JAMIE: [*together*] A whore.

> CLAIRE *gathers her things.*

You can't leave.

CLAIRE: Yes I can.

JAMIE: We haven't finished.

> CLAIRE *throws a fifty at him.*

Whore.

> *He starts masturbating, looking again towards the audience.* CLAIRE *throws another fifty.*

Slut.

> CLAIRE *throws another fifty.*

Cunt.

> CLAIRE *throws the rest of the money at him.*

Death.

CLAIRE: [*quietly*] Boong.

JAMIE *looks at her.*

Boong. Boong. Boong. [*Her voice gets louder and louder.*] Fucking good-for-nothing black bastard. You filthy, drunk, abo pig. Nigger! Nigger! Fucking, filthy, dirty, lazy nigger.

JAMIE *climaxes. He takes the money lying around him and holds it out to* CLAIRE.

JAMIE: Here. Take it. It's yours.

CLAIRE *hesitates. She reaches forward.* JAMIE *holds the money back.*

What are you?

CLAIRE: A whore.

JAMIE *hands her a fifty.*

JAMIE: What are you?

CLAIRE: A slut.

JAMIE *hands her another fifty.*

JAMIE: What are you?

CLAIRE: A cunt.

He holds the rest of the money.

JAMIE: What are you?

CLAIRE: Death.

JAMIE *gives her the money. She pulls on it and he holds on to it.*

JAMIE: Say thanks.

CLAIRE: Thanks.

JAMIE: Thanks…?

CLAIRE: Thanks, sir.

JAMIE *throws the money at her.*

JAMIE: Get out.

He closes his eyes and lies back in bed. CLAIRE *takes the money, adjusts her clothes, walks to the front of the stage and applies her make-up. She takes a fifty-dollar bill and spits on it. She walks out of the room with the money in her hand.*

There is a knock on the door. JAMIE *is still. The knock is repeated.* JAMIE *doesn't move. A final knock.* JAMIE *waits. He switches the mobile phone on and sits upright on the bed, tense, waiting. The mobile phone rings.*

◆ ◆ ◆ ◆ ◆

DREAM-TOWN

SCENE ONE

A changing room.

TRISHA *and* KATINA *are both about fifteen. Neither of them are Anglo, but they are not from the same cultural background. They are jammed together into a tiny changing room in a big department store. They are in the process of taking off their clothes. A stack of evening dresses is hanging on the hook. Their bags are on the floor. They talk quite fast, overlapping a lot.*

TRISHA: She sweared you know and she's not meant to swear, I mean according to her she's not meant to swear…

KATINA: They all swear… adults… all of them. All the fucking teachers swear.

TRISHA: Yeah, Mr Cameron…

KATINA: Cops swear, shit they swear like…

TRISHA: Yeah.

KATINA: … and then they get people up on a bad language charge, and they are the worst, fuck this, fuck that, they are…

TRISHA: She said you're an embarrassment.

KATINA: Did she?

TRISHA: So I said you're an embarrassment, then she said you are, and I said you are, and she said you are and I said what am I, what am I and she said you're an embarrassment to me, Trisha, a fucking embarrassment.

KATINA: That's bad, man.

TRISHA: Then she pricks me with the pin, right, like on purpose, I'm sure on purpose, that's child cruelty or something, on my arm, look you can still see the mark…

> KATINA *is concentrating on her dress.* TRISHA *inspects the mark and then squeezes it hard to make it bleed.*

It's still bleeding.

KATINA: Do this up.

TRISHA: I might get a tattoo.

KATINA: Trisha…

TRISHA: Breathe in.

KATINA: I think it's too small.

TRISHA: No, no breathe in, breathe in.

KATINA: Trisha, it's too small, I need a twelve.

TRISHA: Got it.

KATINA: Fuck, undo it undo it.

TRISHA: It looks really good.

KATINA: Does it?

TRISHA: Pull your shoulders back. Really suits you.

KATINA: I can't breathe.

TRISHA: Twelve'll be too big.

KATINA: Maybe your mum would take it in for me.

TRISHA: I'm not asking her for anything, I didn't finish telling you.

KATINA: Get it off me.

TRISHA: She pricks me with this pin, right, and I go you're dangerous.

KATINA: Get it off me, get it off me.

TRISHA *undoes her.*

Oh my God.

TRISHA: I go you're dangerous, 'cause she's just pricked me with a pin, right, and she goes back you're dangerous. She can't even think up her own insults. I was just standing there. I say how am I dangerous?

KATINA: We are dangerous.

TRISHA: If we had guns, maybe.

KATINA: I could get a gun, I could get my brother's gun.

TRISHA: I didn't know your brother had a gun.

KATINA: Yeah you do.

TRISHA: When?

KATINA: I told you last year. Don't you remember? When that fat guy followed him home.

TRISHA: Oh yeah.

KATINA: That was freaky, man. He was so big and my brother was so off his face, really gone…

TRISHA: Yeah.

KATINA: … and he hits my brother, and my brother looks at his shirt, his white shirt, and it's covered, right, it's covered in blood, and he just loses it, and he goes inside and he's just lost it, and he gets his gun, brings it out, covered in a football sock and my sister and I, we had to grab him and try and get his gun off him…

TRISHA: The guy that lives above us has a gun, this really old man…

KATINA: It was so frightening, we were both shaking, you know. I don't think anyone should have guns. They're too dangerous. Or only really calm people who don't drink and that, you know.

TRISHA: Yeah.

TRISHA *brings out a little bottle of Jim Beam. She has a swig.*

KATINA: Yeah, well I don't wanna gun. You can't get smashed if you've got a gun. I don't wanta worry I'll go get my gun outta my bottom drawer and kill someone accidentally. [*She has a swig.*] If no one had guns Tu-pac wouldn't have died, Notorious wouldn't have died…

TRISHA: Didn't Tu-pac die of AIDS?

KATINA: Easy E died of AIDS. Tu-pac was killed by Junior Mafia and Notorious.

TRISHA *still looks a little blank.*

Tu-pac killed Junior Mafia in one of his songs and fucked his mother…

TRISHA: What?

KATINA: In the song… they all do that, all the gangster rappers do that, they do everything to each other in songs. So then Junior Mafia and Notorious killed Tu-pac in real life. Then someone from Tu-pac's side killed Notorious. Snoop better not be next. I'm gonna kill someone if Snoop dies.

They have a couple more swigs.

TRISHA: Mum you're dead,
I just shot you in the head.

She looks expectantly at KATINA.

KATINA: Yeah sorta like that, but more poetic, you know.

TRISHA: Like what?

KATINA: I dunno, go listen to the music.

TRISHA *starts taking off the dress.*

I like that one on you.

TRISHA: It's too long.

KATINA: Long's good.

TRISHA: And too black.

KATINA: Yeah everyone kills black. How much is it?

TRISHA *looks at the label.*

TRISHA: Five hundred and forty-nine.

KATINA: The city is such a rip off… you'd get that for a hundred in Coburg, don't you reckon?

They both start putting on new frocks.

TRISHA: I really want a smoke.

KATINA: Yeah. Maybe we could go out and come back in.

TRISHA: We don't want to draw too much attention to ourselves.

KATINA: Nah.

TRISHA: I've brought something for us to wear.

KATINA: What do you mean?

TRISHA: I've brought us a disguise… from home.

KATINA: What, like Batman and Robin?

TRISHA: Wait and see.

KATINA: What is it?

> TRISHA *says nothing.*

What is it?

> *She goes for* TRISHA*'s bag.*

TRISHA: Uh uh uh uh…

> TRISHA *fights her off. They piss themselves laughing.*

VOICE: [*offstage*] How are you going in there?

> *They force themselves to stop laughing.*

KATINA: Aah, we haven't finished choosing yet.

> TRISHA *quietly stands on top of her bag.*

I don't care.

> *They resume trying on clothes.*

TRISHA: We had a guy drop dead in the aisle last Wednesday.

KATINA: Man.

TRISHA: Just keeled over, dead.

KATINA: We've never had anyone die. We had a scare with our salami but no one died.

TRISHA: We've had two, a fat lady by the washing-up detergent, and this guy…

KATINA: Where was he?

TRISHA: Near the tea and coffee.

KATINA: They say it's bad for you… We've got this girl that comes in and buys cat food for her baby.

TRISHA: How do you know it's for her baby?

KATINA: You can tell. She gets that fancy Dine stuff. No one buys that.

TRISHA: Maybe she likes her cat.

KATINA: She hasn't got a cat. You can tell. That's all she buys. Cat food.

TRISHA: Eugh. What does she eat? Does she eat cat food?

KATINA: I don't think she eats much. She smokes. Cartons and cartons. She buys a carton a week.

TRISHA: That's disgusting. She buys cigarettes and she feeds her baby cat food.

KATINA: Probably has to smoke to keep the smell away.

TRISHA: You should report her or something.

KATINA: Who would I report her to?

TRISHA: I dunno.

KATINA: The RSPCA.

They laugh.

TRISHA: I wouldn't do that.

KATINA: I wouldn't either.

TRISHA: No matter how bad it got, I wouldn't do that. I'd pinch stuff.

KATINA: So would I.

TRISHA: I'd go to the Salvos.

KATINA: Would you?

TRISHA: Yeah. I'd ask for money on street corners.

KATINA: I wouldn't do that. No way would I do that. I wouldn't beg.

TRISHA: Shit I would. And I'd ask my friends. Why doesn't she ask her friends?

KATINA: She hasn't got any friends.

TRISHA: What's wrong with her?

KATINA: I dunno.

TRISHA: No friends. That'd be the worst. I'd rather be dead than have no friends.

KATINA: She's weird, you know. It's like she lives in the shopping centre, her and her baby, not buying anything, just going 'round and 'round the different shops. You can walk for miles you know, you can get lost in there, everywhere looks like everywhere else. She's always there. Cat Woman.

TRISHA: That's the sort of thing Liana would do, feed her baby pet food.

KATINA: Yeah… and brag about it.

TRISHA: Those Maori chicks.

KATINA: Yeah… Heddi's all right but.

TRISHA: Yeah Heddi's cool.

KATINA: And Annette, she's okay.

TRISHA: Annette's okay, but her cousin's a bitch. She shouldn't hang 'round with her. Who do you think is tougher, Lebo chicks or Maori chicks?

KATINA: Lebo chicks, easy. Maori girls are bigger you know, act tougher, look really scary, but Lebo girls, they follow through I reckon. Put it like this, I'd rather have a Maori chick for an enemy than a Lebo chick. Any day. Like I am glad Dora is my friend you know. I would not want her as my enemy. She is bad.

TRISHA: She's all right.

KATINA: She held Petra's head down the toilet for two minutes, honest. I was there…

TRISHA: That was a set-up.

KATINA: It was not a set-up. She nearly died, man. She nearly drowned with her head down a toilet bowl.

TRISHA: I actually think Asian girls maybe are the toughest.

KATINA: Nah… they're not so tough.

TRISHA: Ling is tough.

KATINA: She's tough, but she's not tough. That's different. She's not weak, but she's not tough. I would go… Lebo chicks toughest, Maori chicks, Greek chicks, Turkish chicks, Italian chicks, Asian chicks… Skippy chicks.

They look at themselves in the mirror, which is the audience perhaps.

You know that body they found.

TRISHA: Yeah.

KATINA: You know they can't tell how old it is or whether it's a man or a woman.

TRISHA: Yeah.

KATINA: I know about something really weird about that.

TRISHA: What?

KATINA: I know these guys right and they know these guys that are real cunning, like really bad, man, really bad, they call themselves The Keepers.

TRISHA: Who are they?

KATINA: Don't ask me their names or anything, they are really bad news, like even Chris and you know, his cousin.

TRISHA: Kevin.

KATINA: Not Kevin you know, Neal.

TRISHA: Neal!

KATINA: Yeah I know, he's an asshole, he would even give his own brother over to the cops I reckon, that guy, I reckon, even his mother…

TRISHA: He's the sort of guy that would pour petrol over his girlfriend and light her up.

KATINA: Yeah… anyway even Neal is afraid of these guys.

TRISHA: What guys?

KATINA: The Keepers.

TRISHA: Why are they called The Keepers?

KATINA: I dunno. They just call themselves that. Like they have names for everything. It's like they've got their own language.

TRISHA: So what about the body?

KATINA: He reckons it's all bullshit about the body being decomposed, he reckons it's perfect, just a bit puffed up from being in the water for so long.

TRISHA: What water?

KATINA: The river water.

TRISHA: I thought they found it in the city square.

KATINA: No it was definitely in the river, 'cause I saw this thing on *A Current Affair* where it was floating under the bridge next to the station.

TRISHA: You saw that on television?

KATINA: It was a re-enactment. That's how they found it. A whole crowd of them saw it and pulled it out. And on the TV they had this burnt-up sort of dummy thing, but this guy reckons that's all crap, that's it perfect, just all puffed up…

TRISHA: If it's so perfect why can't they tell if it's male or female?

KATINA: That's the weird thing.

TRISHA: What?

KATINA: At first they thought it might be confusing because it was having a sex change, and they got caught in the middle of it you know, half man half woman.

TRISHA: Jesus.

KATINA: But it's not.

TRISHA: What is it then?

KATINA: I'll tell you if you show me this stupid disguise you want us to wear.

TRISHA: I pinched two of Mum's uniforms.

KATINA: What?

TRISHA: We'll walk straight out the store.

KATINA: You're crazy.

TRISHA: I nearly got pinched in here you know. I'm not taking any chances.

KATINA: We'll look like idiots.

TRISHA: We won't.

KATINA: I'm not wearing—

TRISHA: Come on, I told you. What about the body?

KATINA: All right. But don't tell anybody all right. I would be dead. These guys are serious. They are serious, man… [*Pause.*] They don't think it's human tissue.

TRISHA: Bullshit.

KATINA: It's true. I swear. It's true.

TRISHA: Fuck. But it looks human?

> KATINA *nods.*

What was it wearing?

KATINA: Nothing… except shoes.

TRISHA: What sort of shoes?

KATINA: A pair of really mad Nikes.

TRISHA: What, Nikes… from earth?

KATINA: What other sort of Nikes are there?

TRISHA: Shit.

KATINA: Really hot, brand-new, shit-hot Nikes.

TRISHA: Shit.

KATINA: Yeah and this guy reckons one of the cops that found the body pinched the Nikes.

◆ ◆ ◆ ◆ ◆

SUIT

SCENE TWO

JAMIE *walks onto the stage. He faces the audience and puts down his briefcase. He knocks. He walks through.*

JAMIE: Are you Mr O'Manney?

> O'MANNEY *is a harsh voice, of the bush. We may not see the actor on stage.* JAMIE, *when he speaks to* O'MANNEY, *speaks to the audience.*

O'MANNEY: What do you want?

JAMIE: I'm here from Southern United.

O'MANNEY: Yeah?

JAMIE: We know that you've been a valued customer for a number of years and we're concerned you haven't taken out a policy with us this year.

> *There is silence.*

Have you been unhappy with our services, Mr O'Manney?

O'MANNEY: What's your name?

JAMIE: [*extending his hand*] Colin Murdoch. Pleased to meet you. [*He drops his hand.*] So, have we done something wrong?

O'MANNEY: You from Melbourne?

JAMIE: I've been living in Melbourne for a long time now.

O'MANNEY: But where you from?

JAMIE: I was born in Sydney.

O'MANNEY: Where you from really?

JAMIE: Sydney.

O'MANNEY: [*exasperated*] Your people, where they from?

> JAMIE *hesitates.*

What kind of blackfella are you?

JAMIE: Mum and Dad are both from Sydney. Mr O'Manney, please, Mr Elson personally asked me to come and speak to you.

O'MANNEY: Why didn't he come himself?

JAMIE: Mr Elson is a very busy man.

O'MANNEY: So am I.

> *Silence.*

Since you've asked, I'm not happy with your services. Every fucking time I do anything with you mob now, I'm charged another bloody fee.

JAMIE: I know it's hard, Mr O'Manney, but it is standard business practice these days. We have to compete. Our rates are, I believe, pretty reasonable.

But maybe we can sit down and discuss how you can minimise on our charges.

O'MANNEY: By not fucking paying them.

JAMIE: I can talk to Mr Elson.

O'MANNEY: You?

JAMIE: Yes.

O'MANNEY: You talk to Elson?

JAMIE: Yes, Mr O'Manney.

Silence.

O'MANNEY: Aren't you hot in that suit?

JAMIE: I'm pretty comfortable.

O'MANNEY: Loosen the fucking tie at least.

JAMIE: I'm all right.

O'MANNEY: It's hot.

JAMIE: I'm fine, sir.

O'MANNEY: Come on, mate, it's hot. Take off that fucking tie.

JAMIE: I'm fine.

O'MANNEY: Take off your fucking tie!

JAMIE *undoes the knot of his tie, slowly. He loosens it, it hangs long around his neck, but he does not completely take it off.*

JAMIE: I've brought along some documents for you. They explain other policy alternatives that might be more suitable for your needs. As you're aware, the bush is changing really fast. Communications are altering the traditional way we are doing business.

O'MANNEY: What the fuck do you know of the bush?

JAMIE: Nothing.

O'MANNEY: You wouldn't even fucking know about the blackfella in the bush?

JAMIE: I don't think that's an issue pertinent to the business at hand.

O'MANNEY: What is the business at hand?

JAMIE: Your policy.

O'MANNEY: Right. My policy. Well, Mr...? What was it?

JAMIE: Murdoch.

O'MANNEY: Well, Mr Murdoch, you know what my policy is, not to trust you.

JAMIE: I'm sorry to hear that, Mr O'Manney.

O'MANNEY: You make me sick.

JAMIE: I should leave, Mr O'Manney.

O'MANNEY: You're not a blackfella.

JAMIE: I think I should go.

O'MANNEY: Are you a blackfella?

JAMIE: I'm going, Mr O'Manney. I'll suggest another representative to come and see you about this matter.

O'MANNEY: Blackfella in a suit and tie.

JAMIE: Goodbye, Mr O'Manney.

> JAMIE *begins to walk away.*

O'MANNEY: If your ancestors could see you. All dressed up, a monkey, suit and tie. They'd be sick. They'd laugh first then they'd be sick.

> JAMIE *keeps walking away, briefcase in hand.*

Take off your fucking tie, boong!

JAMIE: [*yelling*] Shut the fuck up! You cunt, you ignorant Irish white cunt!

> *Silence.*

[*With his back to the audience*] I don't have any ancestors, Mr O'Manney. Can you understand that? No God, no ancestors, no Dreamtime, no fucking witchetty grubs. No boomerang. No spear. No bone to point. No flying men, no fucking scared sites. Can you understand that, Mr O'Manney?

> *Silence.*

Mr O'Manney?

> JAMIE *turns around and walks to the front of the stage. He looks at the audience. He starts doing up his tie.*

Have you heard the one about the Irishman in the banana warehouse, Mr O'Manney? He got fired for throwing out all the bent ones. [*Laughing*] Just a joke, Mr O'Manney, just breaking the ice. [*He picks up his briefcase and looks through it.*] You see, sir, we have implemented some changes over the last few months that I think you'll find attractive. Are you interested, sir?

> *Silence.*

Is this a bad time? Tell you what, Mr O'Manney, should we make another time? I'm happy to shout you a few drinks after work if you like. Only too happy to.

> *Silence.*

I'll ring you after lunch. Okay?

> *Silence.* JAMIE *takes books out of his briefcase. He holds them out— 'Das Capital' by Karl Marx, 'My Place' by Sally Morgan, a pornographic magazine.*

I'll leave you some of our advertising material, Mr O'Manney. You'll see that we are earning our clients at least, *at least*, 1.25% more than our closest competitor.

He places the items on the front of the stage.

Please read them, Mr O'Manney. All right?

Silence.

All right. We'll talk later.

He picks up his briefcase and walks away. He closes the door behind him.

◆ ◆ ◆ ◆ ◆

TRASH

SCENE ONE

Winter. Night. ORTON *stands in the light of a street lamp. He blows in his hands to keep warm. He's fifteen. His sister* STACEY *sits in the darkness on a low fence, out of the way. She's thirteen.*

STACEY: Orton, I'm bleeding.
ORTON: Yeah?
STACEY: From my 'gina.
ORTON: Fuck… how come?
STACEY: I don't know.

> *Pause… neither knows what to say.*

ORTON: You got to go home, Stace.
STACEY: Yeah… with you.
ORTON: Ssh now… car coming.

They wait as a car slows to a cruise and passes.

STACEY: Gone.
ORTON: He'll come back.
STACEY: No… gone.
ORTON: He'll come back 'round.
STACEY: It's too cold.
ORTON: It's fuckin' not.
STACEY: 'Tis.
ORTON: Shut up, would ya? [*Pause.*] Does it hurt?

STACEY: What?

ORTON: Where you're bleeding?

STACEY: It's sore in my tummy.

ORTON: You're just hungry.

STACEY: Yeah.

ORTON: That's all.

STACEY: Yeah.

ORTON: But where you're bleeding, does it hurt?

STACEY: My 'gina?

ORTON: Yeah.

STACEY: It's all right. Lots of blood though.

ORTON: Fuck, Stacey.

STACEY: It's all right.

ORTON: You got to go home.

STACEY: Yeah… with you.

ORTON: Fuck.

STACEY: It's all right.

ORTON: Ssh now… he's coming back 'round.

STACEY: Orton…

ORTON: Told ya.

STACEY: Orton…

ORTON: Got to go.

STACEY: How long?

ORTON: Not long. Where will you be?

STACEY: Here, I'll be here.

ORTON: You can't wait here, Stacey.

STACEY: It's all right.

ORTON: It's too cold. Go up to the shelter.

STACEY: Nah…

ORTON: Fuck… I got to go, Stacey.

STACEY: How long?

ORTON: [*going*] Go up to the shelter an' tell 'em you're bleeding.

STACEY: I'll wait here…

He's gone.

Orton.

STACEY *sits in the dark and waits.*

❖ ❖ ❖ ❖ ❖

DREAM-TOWN

SCENE TWO

A changing room.

KATINA *and* TRISHA *are still in the changing room. They are dressed in private school uniforms with long socks, hats, blazers and their Nikes. They look very fat, having a couple of evening dresses tucked up underneath their uniforms. They are looking in the mirror (i.e. at the audience). They look very serious. They stay looking for a long moment. Finally* KATINA *looks morbidly at* TRISHA.

TRISHA: You look fine.

KATINA: Why didn't you get ones that fit?

TRISHA: They needed to be big.

KATINA: Do I look real?

TRISHA: You look really real.

KATINA: I want a smoke.

TRISHA: We can have a smoke when we get outside, come on.

KATINA: Fuck.

> *They start to go.*

TRISHA: Wait!

KATINA: What!

TRISHA: … I forgot.

> *She gets two pairs of gloves out of her bag.*

KATINA: What are they?

TRISHA: What do they look like?

KATINA: They don't wear fucking evening gloves…

> *They put the gloves on and look in the mirror.*

I feel sick. This is worse than normal shoplifting.

TRISHA: No it's better.

KATINA: Private school girls pinch stuff too you know.

TRISHA: No they don't, not much, why would they? They've got buckets of money.

KATINA: I feel stupid. I feel stupid in this stuff.

TRISHA: Come on.

KATINA: I'm not going out there. I'm putting my real clothes back on. You can be the private school girl… I'll be your friend.

TRISHA: Private school girls don't have friends like you.

KATINA: Well fuck off then. I'm gonna get changed.

TRISHA: Come on, Katina. It's easy. They're just girls. All you've got to do is act like you're not used to being out without your parents.

KATINA: Your mother is going to kill us.

TRISHA: I don't care. She's a mole.

KATINA: She'll kill us.

TRISHA: She won't find out. I'll just hang them back on the rack. There's hundreds of them.

KATINA: What school do we go to again?

TRISHA: I dunno. On your pocket.

> KATINA *looks at her blazer pocket.*

KATINA: It's in Latin.

TRISHA: Come on. Just act rich.

> TRISHA *feeds* KATINA *a swig of Jim Beam. She takes another swig herself. They exit the cubicle and the space.* KATINA *and* TRISHA *both appear together somewhere else in the space. They scan the scene. They start walking very carefully through the space.* KATINA *staring at the ground.* TRISHA *is gaining in confidence, looking about her.* TRISHA *stops at a make-up counter. She smiles at a shop assistant and picks out a lipstick. She pulls out the reluctant* KATINA*'s arm and tries the shade on her. She tries other shades. Finally she picks one and puts it on* KATINA*'s lips.* KATINA *is starting to relax. They are very intimate and easy with each other. Then* KATINA *paints* TRISHA*'s lips. They both smile at the assistant.* KATINA *wants to go.* TRISHA *picks up a perfume sample, sprays it on her wrist and smells it. She holds it out to* KATINA *to smell.* KATINA *makes a face.* TRISHA *sprays it on both of them and then into the air like air-freshener. They laugh.*

◆ ◆ ◆ ◆ ◆

TRASH

SCENE TWO

Later that night. STACEY *is sitting on the wall.* ORTON *approaches. He carries a plastic 7-11 bag.* STACEY *doesn't say anything.*

ORTON: What's the matter?

> *She doesn't reply.*

Stace?

STACEY: I hate you.

ORTON: You do not.

STACEY: I fuckin' do. I hate ya.

ORTON: I was looking for you.

STACEY: I was here.

ORTON: Yeah but I was looking for you.

STACEY: Where you been?

ORTON: Around.

STACEY: Where you been?

ORTON: Shops.

STACEY: I've been waiting.

ORTON: I told you to go up the shelter.

STACEY: I been waiting here.

ORTON: Fuck, Stacey.

STACEY: You've been gone a long time.

ORTON: I went to the shops.

STACEY: I'm cold.

ORTON: Go home.

STACEY: Yeah… with you.

ORTON: I'm not going home, Stacey. [*Pause.*] Brought you something.

STACEY: What is it?

ORTON: A pie.

He gives STACEY *the pie.*

STACEY: Sauce?

ORTON: Yeah. And here.

He passes STACEY *a pack of Modess.*

STACEY: What is it?

ORTON: It's for the bleeding.

STACEY: But what is it?

ORTON: I don't know. It's for the bleeding. I asked Michelle.

STACEY: You told her?

ORTON: She said to go up and see her and she'll show you what to do.

STACEY: What'd you tell her for?

ORTON: Shit, Stacey.

STACEY: What you tell her for?

ORTON: You're bleeding.

STACEY: So… shouldn't of told you. Shouldn't of said.

ORTON: Is it still happening?

STACEY: I don't know.
ORTON: Is it or isn't it?
STACEY: I don't know.
ORTON: Shit...

STACEY *opens the packet.*

STACEY: What do you do with them?
ORTON: You stick 'em on.
STACEY: Where?
ORTON: Where you're bleeding.
STACEY: My 'gina?
ORTON: Yeah, shit, I don't know. You got to go and see Michelle.
STACEY: She's a bitch.
ORTON: She's all right.
STACEY: She's a bitch, Orton.
ORTON: Then you got to go home.

STACEY *peels off the adhesive tab.*

STACEY: Won't it hurt?
ORTON: I don't know. Stop asking me about it. Read the packet.

STACEY *looks at the packet, trying to make out the instructions.*

What's it say?
STACEY: I don't know.
ORTON: What's it say?
STACEY: I can't read it.

ORTON *snatches the packet and searches it for instructions. There aren't any.*

What's it say?
ORTON: You stick 'em on.
STACEY: Is that what it says?
ORTON: Yeah... kind of.
STACEY: I'm not using them.
ORTON: Go and ask Michelle.
STACEY: I'm not using them.
ORTON: Shit, Stacey... they cost money.
STACEY: I'm not using them.
ORTON: Are you still bleeding?
STACEY: I don't know.
ORTON: You need Mum.
STACEY: Will we go home?

ORTON: I'm not going home.

ORTON *moves back into the light, waiting again for passing cars.*

STACEY: It's late now, Orton.

ORTON: It's not.

STACEY: It's too cold.

ORTON: Cold doesn't matter.

STACEY: There'll be no more cars.

ORTON: That's what you think.

STACEY: Let's go.

ORTON: You go.

STACEY: With you.

ORTON: You go.

STACEY: You come too.

ORTON: Not yet.

STACEY: 'T's cold.

ORTON: Fuck, Stacey. It's cold. That's all you say.

STACEY: But it is.

ORTON: You shouldn't have come looking for me.

STACEY: Found you though.

ORTON: I didn't ask you to.

STACEY: Told Mum I would.

ORTON: She'll be worried.

STACEY: Nah.

ORTON: She'll call the police.

STACEY: She won't. She fucking won't, Orton, and you know it.

ORTON: She shouldn't have let you come. She shouldn't.

STACEY: Told her I'd find you.

ORTON: That was three nights ago, Stace.

STACEY: She wants you to come home.

ORTON: I'm not. You go home and you tell her that. You go home and tell her you found me and I'm not coming home. Ever. Go on.

STACEY: Not without you.

ORTON: Fuck you. You're stupid, you know. I can't look after you.

STACEY: Don't have to.

ORTON: I don't want you with me. Fuck off. Go on. [*He runs at her.*] Go on. I'll fucking hit you. I fucking will.

STACEY *moves away. He throws something at her.*

Fuck off.

STACEY *has moved out of sight.* ORTON *moves back under the street lamp and waits. After a moment* STACEY *returns and sits back on the wall.* ORTON *knows she's there but doesn't look.*

❖ ❖ ❖ ❖ ❖

MONEY

SCENE TWO: TRAIN

The MAN *is in a suit and he carries a briefcase. He is travelling on the train, on his way to work. Another passenger, a* MUSICIAN, *may sit quietly playing.*

A YOUNG WOMAN *boards the train. She is dressed in a very short skirt and wears a lot of make-up. She sits opposite the* MAN. *She looks out the window for a while until she notices the* MAN *staring at her. She tries to ignore him but the intensity of his gaze annoys her.*

GIRL: What are you looking at?
MAN: You.
GIRL: Don't.

> *He continues to stare.*

Stop staring at me.
MAN: You sat opposite me.
GIRL: I sat opposite you.
MAN: You had all these seats to choose from and you chose to sit opposite me.
GIRL: So? What's your point?
MAN: If you didn't want me to look at you, why sit opposite me?

> *She runs the following lines on over his.*

GIRL: Oh my God, you think I'm coming on to you.
MAN: No I don't.
GIRL: You think I sat opposite you so that I could come on to you.
MAN: No I don't.
GIRL: You think I got up this morning and into these clothes so that I could come on to you.
MAN: That's not what I think.
GIRL: Why would I do that? Do you think I saw you from the platform and thought, ooh, there's a fine-looking bloke and he's all alone. I'm going to come on to him.
MAN: No...

GIRL: No that's right, I just happen to be fucking sitting opposite you.

MAN: There's no reason for you to use that language.

GIRL: I'll use whatever fucking language I like.

MAN: I'm asking you nicely, I find your swearing offensive and I would appreciate it if you'd stop.

GIRL: Why?

MAN: You are genuinely asking me why?

GIRL: Yes. Why?

MAN: Because it makes you look stupid and cheap.

GIRL: No it doesn't.

MAN: I'm telling you it does.

GIRL: You telling me doesn't make it true. I think my swearing makes you look stupid and a dickhead.

MAN: You speak like that and you'll never get anywhere.

GIRL: And where would that be?

MAN: You won't get a job with a mouth on you like that.

GIRL: I'm not going to get a job.

MAN: Not looking like that.

GIRL: Like what?

MAN: The way you're dressed.

GIRL: What way's that?

MAN: I'm telling you if you came to me and asked me for work looking like that, there is no way I would consider you. You wouldn't even get in the door.

GIRL: Looking like what?

MAN: The way you're dressed.

GIRL: Yes?

MAN: Like that. Like you are.

GIRL: Don't worry about it, I wouldn't come to you.

MAN: No one else would consider you either.

GIRL: Don't worry about it, it's got nothing to do with you.

MAN: Look at your hair.

GIRL: What about it?

MAN: How do you expect to get on looking like that?

GIRL: I get on fine.

MAN: You get on fine, do you? Get on fine? How's that? You don't work.

GIRL: No, I don't.

MAN: Have you ever worked?

GIRL: No, I haven't.

MAN: And you get on fine. You on the dole? Yeah, you get on fine.

GIRL: Me not getting a job has nothing to do with my hair or what I wear.

MAN: No. How do you know? Maybe it has, maybe it hasn't. How do you know if you never give it a go?

GIRL: How do you know I haven't?

MAN: How old are you? Twenty-three, twenty-four, something like that?

GIRL: Something like that.

MAN: You're like my son Daniel.

GIRL: Oh no, you have a son.

MAN: You think you've got time on your hands. You probably think something will come up, something's sure to happen. It's as clear as day what'll happen to you. Nothing. Maybe you think you won't have to work, that some bloke will look after you, lavish you with gifts, set you up in a nice house. No bloke's going do that, not with you looking like that he's not.

GIRL: And you'd know?

MAN: Do you want to be anything? Got any dreams, any hopes, any desires to do something with yourself?

GIRL: Not really.

MAN: Nothing you want? Not one small dream hiding away somewhere?

GIRL: No.

MAN: You're perfectly happy with who you are?

GIRL: Yeah, that's right.

MAN: I don't believe you.

GIRL: Who asked you to?

MAN: I bet you have lots of dreams. I bet you think that one day, one day soon, someone, someone important, some producer or director, or a talent scout, is going to see you and think, wow, here she is, here's the one we've been looking for, she's just right, she's perfect and before you know it, you'll be whisked away and put on some teleseries and before you know it your face will be in every magazine and it will be all so glamorous, and every one of us will be screaming and asking for your autograph. And the next thing you know you'll put out a hit single and then a CD and you'll be off touring the world, as famous as can be, and rich, so rich you won't know what to do with it. Am I right, am I close? One day, one day soon, someone, someone important, will come along and take you away from all this.

The GIRL *is uncomfortable.*

I'm sure you have a few dreams like that.

GIRL: No I don't.

MAN: And who knows, dreams do sometimes come true. Who knows, of all the girls dreaming that exact dream, maybe it will be you who'll be spotted. Who knows? Maybe, it will be a girl like you.

GIRL: A girl like me?

MAN: It doesn't seem likely, does it? Not looking the way you look.

The GIRL *gets up to move to a different seat. She bumps the briefcase from the* MAN*'s knees and it falls open to the floor. It is empty. The* MAN *and the* GIRL *bend to pick it up and each rise holding either side of it.*

GIRL: What's this? What's going on here?

She continues to hold on to the case although he struggles to take it from her.

It's empty.

MAN: Let go of my briefcase.

GIRL: It's empty. Not a thing. Not even a sandwich.

MAN: Would you let go of my fucking briefcase.

GIRL: Your fucking briefcase is empty!

MAN: So fucking what!

GIRL: You'll never get anywhere speaking like that.

She lets go of the case.

You haven't got a job!

MAN: Don't be ridiculous. Of course I've got a job.

GIRL: Look at the way you're dressed. Look at your hair. Look at your cuffs. They're frayed. And your suit needs a dry clean. Your hair needs a cut. I wouldn't consider giving you a job looking like that. You wouldn't even get in the door.

MAN: I've got a job.

GIRL: Had one maybe. But you haven't got one anymore.

MAN: I assure you, I am working. I've had the same job for fifteen years.

GIRL: Let's have a look at your shoes?

MAN: [*withdrawing his feet*] There is no need for you to look at my shoes.

GIRL: Don't be shy, show me your shoes.

The GIRL *bends down to look at his shoes.*

MAN: Leave my shoes alone!

GIRL: [*laughing*] You haven't got a job.

MAN: I have. Of course I have.

GIRL: You're full of shit.

MAN: Don't be ridiculous.

GIRL: You've lost it.

MAN: No, I'm working.

GIRL: Got too old? Got too slow?

MAN: I told you I'm working.

GIRL: Maybe you had a dream, took a chance, gave up your stuffy old job, in a bank I reckon. Took a package! Thought, now's my chance to be my own man, to make something of myself, to be my own boss. Maybe of an ice-cream van or maybe one of those Jims with their mowers. That's the life for me, you thought. And now you're on the same train as me.

MAN: I've got a job!

GIRL: And now you want your job back. But the job is gone.

The MAN *pulls out a wad of money.*

MAN: How would I have money like this if I didn't have a job?

GIRL: Better buy a suit, better get a haircut because you're never going to get anywhere looking like that.

MAN: You're so smart, aren't you? [*Pause.*] At least I had a job. I worked for fifteen years. That's got to mean something. [*Pause.*] Don't you think?

GIRL: What?

MAN: It's got to mean something.

GIRL: What?

MAN: The fifteen years.

GIRL: What's it got to mean? Who's it got to mean something to? Who gives a shit?

MAN: Says you who hasn't worked a fucking hour in your whole fucking life.

GIRL: It's got to mean something that I've never worked an hour in my fucking life. What? What's it got to mean. Nothing. To no one. Who gives a shit?

◆ ◆ ◆ ◆ ◆

TRASH

SCENE THREE

Later that night. The sea wall. ORTON *and* STACEY *stand on the wall looking out over the water. There's a jetty trailing out into the darkness.* STACEY *holds her 7-11 bag. There's a heavy fog sitting above black water.*

ORTON: You see that, Stace?

STACEY: Yeah.

ORTON: They say when the fog sits above the water like that it's the suicide night.

STACEY: Why?

ORTON: 'Cause it's warmer in than out.

STACEY: It's not. No way. Nobody says that, Orton.

ORTON: They say when it's so cold that the ocean steams somebody on the street's gonna deck themselves.

They see a figure standing at the end of the jetty. It's JAMIE. ORTON *watches him on and off through the scene.*

STACEY: In the car? What do you do?

ORTON: Nothing.

STACEY: For the money.

ORTON: It doesn't matter.

STACEY: Do you suck 'em?

ORTON: Yeah, that and other stuff.

STACEY: And they give you money?

ORTON: Yeah.

STACEY: How much?

ORTON: Quit talking 'bout it.

STACEY: But how much?

ORTON: Depends.

STACEY: Depends on what?

ORTON: On what you do.

STACEY: That's like Nathan.

ORTON: How do you mean?

STACEY: That's what Nathan was like.

ORTON: What?

STACEY: But he didn't give me any money.

Pause… as ORTON *takes this in.*

ORTON: Did you tell Mum?

STACEY: Yeah. When he first did it.

ORTON: What'd she say?

STACEY: That's when she said I had to sleep in your room.

ORTON: That was years ago, Stace. When you came into my room that was years ago. It was Phil then, not Nathan.

STACEY: You were pissed off.

ORTON: She didn't tell me.

STACEY: You wanted your own room.

ORTON: But she didn't tell me why.

STACEY: It doesn't matter.

ORTON: She should have told me, Stace. You should have.

STACEY: She said 'don't tell'. [*Pause.*] Who's Phil?

ORTON: Phil was before Nathan.

STACEY: I don't remember him.

ORTON: Yes you do, you just don't remember his name.

STACEY: Was Phil better than Nathan?

ORTON: Same.

STACEY: Same as Nathan?

ORTON: Yeah.

STACEY: But there was someone who was good.

ORTON: Teddy. You were little.

STACEY: He was good.

ORTON: Yeah.

STACEY: To Mum.

ORTON: Yeah. He was Mickey's dad.

STACEY: Who?

ORTON: Don't forget, Stace. You shouldn't forget. Our little brother, his name's Mickey.

STACEY: But what happened to Teddy?

ORTON: I don't know.

STACEY: And where's Mickey?

ORTON: Welfare's got him.

JAMIE *is walking along the path toward them.*

JAMIE: [*as he passes*] What are you looking at?

ORTON: Nothing.

JAMIE *walks on and disappears into the mist.* ORTON *watches him go.* STACEY *stares out over the water.*

STACEY: Anyway… I'd rather burn than drown.

ORTON: Yeah… me too.

❖ ❖ ❖ ❖ ❖

DREAM-TOWN

LEON MONOLOGUE

LEON *is sitting by himself in his house. His left hand is bandaged.*

February four years ago, it was still Spring, metaphorically speaking, in the Pragueian sense of the word, before the tanks rolled in. I am a wood-turner by trade and I am also what is known as an autodidact. Terry Lane called me that in our first telephone conversation. I took it as a compliment. I was still making tables in the spring but things got very stressful and I hurt my hand. I don't know if I hurt my hand because things were stressful, or if things got stressful because I hurt my hand. I'm being intimate with you now. I'm being honest. Don't fuck this up. I was given money for three months, but my hand didn't get better. I won't go into the details of my hand injury, but believe me, it got no better, and around this time I became a single man again and people aren't made to be single, they rot away inside, and I was rotting and my hand was rotting and they argued over whether I was a physical injury or psychologically damaged, every week a different version, every week another set of guidelines, then Winter followed Spring and they took away the money. That was the start of the troubles. I didn't ring the radio during this time. I want that to be absolutely crystal clear. I rang no one but the WorkCover people and spoke a couple of times to my wife's mother who is a woman of some sympathy, unlike my wife. That is the truth. It was around this time that they dropped the twos. One-cent pieces had been dropped a long time before. I had very little money, understand this, and I saw a fatal gap in the system, a little Eureka at the Coles supermarket. Because Coles, unlike Safeway, or Woolworths, had decided to mark down. If a kilo of carrots costs a dollar twenty-five, a single carrot, weighing one gram, will cost four cents. At a Coles supermarket, rounded down, the carrot will cost nothing. It was totally legal, and I had nothing else to do. I spent days in the supermarket, putting through purchases one by one. And contrary to what people may say, I saved money. Sizeable amounts of money when judged in relation to my income. And then they cracked down on me. Mr Carpazzier, the manager, banned me and it was only then I started ringing people to tell my story. They loved me at first, the media jackals, they couldn't get enough of me. 'Oh it's Leon', they'd say, 'Stay on the line, Leon, give your number to the producer'. They loved me and my strange little story, and I loved them, all of them. While it was happening I couldn't see it ever stopping. I thought I was permanently established as someone to whom people would come to for a particular view of the world, like a famous historian or a respected economist. But to stay famous and important you have to shut up. Fame is shit. Fame is all about lies and compromise, and because I didn't keep my mouth shut, they dropped me. The black death. See I know secret things, I know things that could blast you out of the water, things that will only get revealed after the twenty-five-year silence, the little scam they're running at the National Library in Canberra. That's where they keep all the secrets. It's all lies, the lot of it, all lies. I can't watch television anymore. It makes me vomit, physically it makes me sick. It's not my cigarettes, it's not the coffee or the Panadeine for my constant headache. I used to watch all the current affairs shows. Way back. Way back in the Golden Age. Jana Wendt, she was gorgeous, she was like a whip, a frozen whip, but they got rid of her. I wrote to her during the troubles but she never answered, they censored her mail. If Jana had got hold of my story it would have been on every front page in every fucking paper, she's got integrity. She's got lips that smile with the wisdom of the ages, and eyes that tell of all the horrors of the twentieth century. She hasn't got a sense of humour, not exactly, but she's got irony, wit and irony, not like all those dumb bimbos they get on the other stations, they get rid of all the strong ones. Jill Singer, that was another one. They shaft 'em, they push the dagger in right up to the hilt and they twist it and twist it and we're all left fucking bleeding.

I've rung them all.

I've rung Bruce and Phyll and Ernie and Eddie.

Steve and Ross and Kevin and Yvonne.

I've rung Neil Mitchell, he called me a psychopath.

I've rung McGowan in the middle of the night, countless times. They don't let me through. He hates my guts and I hate his.

I've rung Delroy, Faine, Lane and all the other ABC assholes… They all talk like headmasters, and they're all fucking Christians, have you noticed that, all ex-seminarians, but do they let a man have his say? Jesus would have rung up the ABC and had his little twenty-second grab on the 'gripe-line', until he said that Herod was a fuck-wit and then he'd be gone and the little girl on the switchboard would tell the producer who'd warn the presenter and you'd never be on air again. 'Cause they're all scared of Herod really. Little 'fraidy cats, fucking ABC 'fraidy cats…

I don't ring anymore, not much. I'm studying. The fall of the Roman Empire, Suetonius, Tacitus, Dio Cassius, Seneca… the philosophers. I especially enjoy the philosophers…

◆ ◆ ◆ ◆ ◆

MONEY

SCENE THREE: BREAK-IN

The scene begins in darkness, only a dimly-lit window in view. The BOY *(*DANIEL*) comes to the outside of the window and peers through. He jemmies the window open and climbs into the dark room. It is sparsely furnished with a bed and bookshelves. A body in the bed stirs and an* OLD WOMAN *sits up. They frighten each other. They are still with fright for a long time.*

OLD WOMAN: Jimmy, is that you?

> DANIEL *bolts for the window and is about to leave through it.*

Jimmy, don't go. Don't go!

> *He climbs down from the ledge and re-enters the room.*

Oh Jimmy, it's good to see you.

DANIEL: [*tentatively*] I didn't know anyone was here.

OLD WOMAN: Yes, I'm here. [*Confused*] What am I doing here?

DANIEL: I don't know. [*Pause.*] Are you sick?

OLD WOMAN: No, I'm well. Least I think I'm well.

DANIEL: Maybe you're tired.

OLD WOMAN: Maybe that's it. I'm tired. Yes, that must be it. I have been tired lately. But I'm not tired now, seeing you. Here, help me, help me up.

> DANIEL *remains still.*

What is it, Jimmy? Help me. I want to get you something to eat. You must be hungry.

DANIEL: I'm not hungry.

OLD WOMAN: Come here, Jimmy, I can't see you there. Come here.

DANIEL: No!

OLD WOMAN: What is it, Jimmy?

DANIEL: I'm not who you think I am.

OLD WOMAN: You're my Jimmy.

DANIEL: I'm not. You don't know me.

OLD WOMAN: I know you.

DANIEL: You don't know me.

OLD WOMAN: You're my son.

DANIEL: I'm not your son.

OLD WOMAN: And you've come back.

DANIEL: I don't know you.

OLD WOMAN: Of course you know me, you're my son.

DANIEL: I'm not.

OLD WOMAN: I'm your mother and you're my son and that's final.

DANIEL: [*stepping closer to the* OLD WOMAN] Look at me. Is this the face of your son?

OLD WOMAN: [*slowly putting her hand to his cheek*] Jimmy? Oh, you've come back my beautiful boy.

DANIEL: [*pulling away*] I'm not your bloody Jimmy, you stupid bloody… I'm here to rob you.

OLD WOMAN: To rob me? Take what you want. What's mine is yours.

Pause.

DANIEL: Where's your purse?

OLD WOMAN: My purse. Now where would I have put my purse? [*She rummages in the bed looking for it.*] I can't seem to find it. Put on the light, Jimmy.

DANIEL *attempts to turn the switch but nothing happens.*

I've found it. How much do you need?

DANIEL: All of it. Give me all of it. [*He takes the purse.*] Is this it? There's only a couple of dollars in it.

OLD WOMAN: Is there? I'm sure I had more than that.

DANIEL: Where? Where else do you keep your money?

OLD WOMAN: Maybe there's a hole in the purse.

DANIEL: You must have money somewhere. How else do you pay your bills? [*He looks at the light switch.*] Oh shit! Shit! You don't. You don't pay them.

OLD WOMAN: I pay all my bills and always before time. You know me better than that. Look in my bookshelves. Over there, in that big book, *Das Kapital*. I used to hide some money in the leaves. See if there's any there. There, the big red one.

DANIEL *finds the book and fans its pages.*

DANIEL: Nothing. What about other stuff? Jewellery, stuff like that? Show us your hands. Where's your rings?

OLD WOMAN: Never worn a ring in my life.

DANIEL: I'm a loser. I'm trying to rob you and you've got less than me.

OLD WOMAN: You're not a loser, Jimmy.

DANIEL: I am not Jimmy. I don't live here. I have a mother.

OLD WOMAN: Your mother is dead.

DANIEL: Yeah right.

OLD WOMAN: Your mother died in childbirth. I got you from the Banyule orphanage when you were six weeks old. I took you home and I looked after you. I clothed you, I fed you, I sent you to school. You never wanted for anything. And I loved you as if you were truly mine. Your real mother is dead.

DANIEL: But I'm not Jimmy. My mother isn't dead.

OLD WOMAN: She is. [*In a whisper*] I'm sorry, Jimmy, but it's for the best.

DANIEL: My mother isn't dead!

OLD WOMAN: Sshh, Jimmy. Sshh! She's gone. I'm sorry to have to tell you like this but you had to know.

DANIEL: Look, my name is… forget my name. You think I'm your son.

OLD WOMAN: You are my son.

DANIEL: That's what I'm trying to tell you. I'm not. No, listen to me. I have a mother. And a father for that matter.

OLD WOMAN: Father unknown.

DANIEL: My mother—

OLD WOMAN: Dead.

DANIEL: She was far from it when I saw her this morning.

Pause.

OLD WOMAN: You saw her?

DANIEL: This morning.

Pause.

OLD WOMAN: I told her to keep away from you. I told her, what was the point? Leave it alone. What good could it do? You'll bring him heartache I said. He doesn't need you. You left him. I'm his mother now, not you.

DANIEL: You lied.

OLD WOMAN: No…

DANIEL: You did. You lied. You told him she was dead.

OLD WOMAN: It was for the best.

DANIEL: Lies are never for the best.

OLD WOMAN: She couldn't look after you.

DANIEL: You sent her away.

OLD WOMAN: She was only a girl, unmarried… What could she offer you? You would have had no education to speak of.

DANIEL: Maybe she just wanted to see him. That's all. Just have a look at him.

OLD WOMAN: Give you back because you're of the same blood. A load of nonsense. I offered you a world worth fighting for.

DANIEL: It was based on lies.

OLD WOMAN: It was based on a bigger picture where greater things are at stake than family and blood ties and small miseries that are not worth their salt.

DANIEL: You told him his mother's dead and then she turns up. How did you expect him to feel?

OLD WOMAN: I expected you to recognise what I had done for you.

DANIEL: Well, it fucked up, didn't it, because he's not here.

OLD WOMAN: I didn't want to lose you.

DANIEL: You did.

OLD WOMAN: You were mine.

DANIEL: No! I wasn't... I'm not. You should've... This is not... Look, I'm not... You're not... Fuck this! I'm out of here.

OLD WOMAN: No! Please don't go! Don't go, Jimmy.

DANIEL: I am not Jimmy!

OLD WOMAN: I promise I won't call you Jimmy anymore, only please don't go.

DANIEL: I'm only here to rob you. You must have something that's worth something.

OLD WOMAN: I wish I did and I could give it to you. If I did I could say, here, get what you need, look after yourself, make yourself happy. There must be something I can give you. What about my books? Could you sell them? There's plenty of them.

    DANIEL *looks at the books and laughs.*

DANIEL: I am such a loser.

OLD WOMAN: There's nothing loser about you. I knew that the moment I saw you. You're going to be something one day.

DANIEL: I'm going to be nothing.

OLD WOMAN: I look at you and you make it seem worthwhile.

DANIEL: Yeah, but it's not me you're looking at.

OLD WOMAN: You're lovely.

DANIEL: I'm not fucking lovely.

OLD WOMAN: You're strong. You're as smart as they come.

DANIEL: I'm a fucking genius.

OLD WOMAN: I look at you and I don't feel despair anymore. You're here. You'll carry on. You're a good boy.

DANIEL: Yeah I'm so good. I've broken into your house. I've pocketed the only three dollars you've got. I would have bloody ripped your fingers off if you had any rings on them. I'm real good! You don't know me.

OLD WOMAN: You need the money. If you had some I'm sure you wouldn't bother. There's nothing wrong with you. I can see that in your eyes. Such lovely eyes. There's no deceit, no greed.

DANIEL: You don't know anything about me.

OLD WOMAN: What do I need to know? That you're bad? I don't think so.

DANIEL: [*very quietly*] I am not your Jimmy.

> *Silence. They look at one another.*

My name is Daniel.

OLD WOMAN: It suits you.

> DANIEL *goes to the window.*

DANIEL: I could call someone.

OLD WOMAN: No. Thank you, but no.

> DANIEL *leaves.*

◆ ◆ ◆ ◆ ◆

DREAM-TOWN

SCENE THREE

A police station.

TRISHA *and* KATINA *are sitting in chairs, in their uniforms and their stolen dresses, facing a bored* COP. TRISHA *is scared and defiant. The* COP *looks at* TRISHA.

COP ONE: Name?

> TRISHA *says nothing.*

Gonna tell me your name?

> TRISHA *says nothing. The* COP *looks at* KATINA.

What about you?

KATINA: Carol.

COP ONE: Carol what?

KATINA: Carol Kennett.

COP ONE: Carol Kennett.

KATINA: Ahuh… yeah.

COP ONE: Don't bullshit me.

KATINA: That's my name.

COP ONE: Any relation to the Premier?

KATINA: Who? Oh no, no relation… we spell it differently.

COP ONE: How do you spell it?

KATINA: K, E, double-N, E, double-T.

COP ONE: That's how he spells it.

KATINA: Is it? Well he might be a relation you know… Really distant. He doesn't come 'round to visit.

COP ONE: And what's her name?

KATINA: I can't tell you if she doesn't want to tell you, can I? She's probably got very strong reasons for doing what she's doing.

COP ONE: What's your name?

The COP *stares at* TRISHA.

TRISHA: I don't have to say anything. You're not even meant to be asking us questions without our parents here. You're not even meant to be in the same room with us without our parents here.

COP ONE: Well you tell me who your parents are.

TRISHA: I don't have to tell you anything.

COP ONE: What school do you go to?

TRISHA *says nothing.* KATINA*'s eyes start snaking down towards her pocket.*

KATINA: Mena Civis.

COP ONE: What?

KATINA: Mena Civis school.

COP ONE: Never heard of it.

KATINA: Haven't you?

COP ONE: What's it's called again?

KATINA: Mena Civis school.

COP ONE: How do you spell that?

KATINA *looks down at her pocket.*

KATINA: M, E, N, A. C, I, V, I, S. S, C, H—

COP ONE: I know how to spell school.

KATINA: Yeah it's very exclusive you know.

COP ONE: Some sort of fancy alternative school, is it?

KATINA: Yeah something like that. I'm afraid my parents are out of town at the moment, I could give you their names and stuff but... you know... they're OS. They're foreign diplomats, you know with the Government...

COP ONE: Both of them.

KATINA: Yeah both of them, a sort of husband and wife team, they're inseparable, they hate being apart you know. Like Mulder and Scully you know, in the *X-Files*, except my parents are married... and not that young...

COP ONE: So where exactly are they?

KATINA: America actually, at the moment, sort of West Coast, sometimes they take us with them but this time, no way, it'd be too dangerous, too much violence, too many gangsters... people killing each other all the time, stuff like that you know. They thought it would be better if I stayed here, me and my brother and sisters, nice and safe, with my... nanny.

COP ONE: You've got a nanny.

KATINA: Yeah, I got a nanny… she's fabulous… she's sort of um real crazy you know, dresses really well… she's Jewish… We sort of talked about boarding school… that was the other sort of, possibility. I thought it might be okay for a while you know, sort of fun you know like camping out or something, but just too many girls. I've always got on better with the boys, you know, played in their playground.

COP ONE: So why were you stealing, Carol?

KATINA: Well… it's sort of hard to explain… [*She fingers the evening dress.*] Nanny's been really sick. She's had a nervous breakdown… I don't know if it was the strain of looking after us, or other things in her personal life… I don't know… but she shakes, you know, she drinks… that was her Jim Beam in the bag, I had to confiscate it from her, she's disgusting you know and she just won't get out of bed to go to the bank and so I haven't had any of the money that my parents left with her for me and my brother and sisters. My brother thinks she may have actually gambled it all away. He saw her coming out of one of those pokie clubs… Tabaret, you know, which is terrible… he says she lives in them, just sits all day on the ten-cent machines, they just eat up money you know… it's just terrible, my parents would just die to know they left us in the trusted care of an alcoholic and a gambler.

COP ONE: Why don't you just ring them up?

KATINA: They're undercover.

COP ONE: Spies you mean?

KATINA: I'm not meant to talk about it sorry… so anyway… we've been living on nothing you know, having to steal everything, just to survive… the washing machine broke and we didn't have enough money to fix it… it's been a real eye-opener for me I can tell you and you know it's given me a real insight into how the other half lives… I think now when I grow up I might work with the poor. I've been very selfish in my life you know, very sheltered… haven't probably seen a lot of the real world. It's been very easy for me you know. I was going to be a lawyer, my parents have a lot of lawyer friends who could get me jobs… but in the last week or two after all this heartache and hardship I've completely changed my mind.

COP ONE: What are you going to be now?

KATINA: Probably a social worker I reckon, or a prison warder…

❖ ❖ ❖ ❖ ❖

TRASH

SCENE FOUR

Inside a Brotherhood bin. Darkness.

STACEY: Warm in here.
ORTON: Yeah.
STACEY: Smells but.
ORTON: It's the clothes.

> ORTON *lights a candle. It's a confined space. Clothes spill from plastic bags.*

STACEY: [*holding up an elaborate girl's dress*] Check this.
ORTON: Take it if you want.
STACEY: Nah.
ORTON: Look good on you.
STACEY: [*sardonically*] Yeah sure, Orton.
ORTON: Would.
STACEY: [*rummaging*] Find something for Mum though, ay.
ORTON: Yeah.
STACEY: Take it home for her.
ORTON: You can.
STACEY: [*holding something up like a taffeta ballgown*] Like this.
ORTON: Yeah.
STACEY: Look good on her.
ORTON: Yeah, and I mean she goes to balls all the time like.
STACEY: [*laughing*] Yeah… [*Pause.*] If you could choose, like, where you could live, like with Mum or with a foster family, what would you choose, like what would be the order?
ORTON: The street first.
STACEY: But I mean not counting that.
ORTON: I'd choose Mum, on her own.
STACEY: Me too. That's what I'd choose.
ORTON: And then Mum and Teddy and Mickey.
STACEY: And me.
ORTON: Yeah and you.
STACEY: And then foster.
ORTON: Yeah.
STACEY: Me too.
ORTON: But it depends.

STACEY: Yeah, like on who you get.

ORTON: Yeah.

STACEY: 'Cause some of them are bastards.

ORTON: But some of them are cool.

STACEY: Yeah… like the ones with the pool, they were cool.

ORTON: What pool?

STACEY: That was so cool.

ORTON: I wasn't with you at that place.

STACEY: And then Mum and Nathan. Or Mum and Phil.

ORTON: Nathan and Phil are the same.

STACEY: Yeah but Nathan hits.

ORTON: So did Phil.

STACEY: Not as much though.

ORTON: No.

STACEY: Only when he was really pissed.

ORTON: Yeah.

STACEY: I remember him now.

ORTON: So was he the one doing it to you or Nathan?

STACEY: Both.

ORTON: Fuck, Stace.

Pause.

STACEY: So that's my order.

ORTON: That's my order too.

STACEY: So what about your dad?

ORTON: What about him?

STACEY: You don't look black.

ORTON: A bit.

STACEY: Yeah… a bit. Would you live with him?

ORTON: Yeah, I reckon it'd be all right.

STACEY: You're lookin' for him, aren't you?

ORTON: Yeah.

STACEY: How you going to find him?

ORTON: I don't know.

STACEY: Do you know his name?

ORTON: Yeah.

STACEY: What is it?

ORTON: Jimmy.

STACEY: If you go and live with him, do you think I can live with him too?

ORTON: I don't know. Maybe.

STACEY: But I'm not his daughter.

ORTON: Maybe it wouldn't matter.

STACEY: Do you reckon?

ORTON: I don't know, Stace. I've never met him. Not as if I can go up to him and say me and my sister want to move in.

STACEY: So where would he go on your list though?

ORTON: He'd go after Mum.

STACEY: So it'd go Mum on her own first then your dad.

ORTON: Yeah.

STACEY: Then Mum and Teddy and… [*not remembering*]?

ORTON: Mickey.

STACEY: Mickey.

ORTON: Yeah… I don't know, Stace. Quit asking questions.

STACEY: I'd go Mum on her own first then Mum with Teddy then your dad then—

ORTON: Stace, that's enough. Don't talk about it anymore.

> ORTON *stares into the flame. The lights rise to reveal* RHONDA. *She's sitting on a chair in a bare waiting room. She has a packet of cheap cigarettes. She's constantly playing with it, taking out a cigarette, putting it back in. Her clothes are cheap and her hair unkempt. She looks like what she is, poor white trash. She's several months pregnant, just beginning to show.*

STACEY: What you see in the flame, Orton?

ORTON: Nothing.

STACEY: Our mum…

> ORTON *doesn't reply.*

Just play, Orton, all right. It's our mum, isn't it?

ORTON: Yeah.

STACEY: What's she doing?

ORTON: Nothing.

STACEY: What'ya see though?

ORTON: She's waiting.

STACEY: Yeah…? For us?

ORTON: Yeah.

STACEY: What she wearing?

ORTON: Her good dress.

STACEY: The blue one?

ORTON: Yeah.

STACEY: She going out?

ORTON: Yeah.

STACEY: And her earrings?

> ORTON *nods.*

She got earrings on, Orton?

ORTON: Yeah.

STACEY: She's going out.

ORTON: Looks like it.

STACEY: We'll wait up for her.

ORTON: She'll be late.

STACEY: Doesn't matter. We'll wait up.

ORTON: She'll come home pissed.

STACEY: Will not.

ORTON: She fuckin' will.

STACEY: Doesn't matter.

ORTON: She's a bitch.

STACEY: You shut up, Orton. You fucking shut up. 'Cause she's not. It doesn't matter. Nothing. It doesn't matter. None of it. You hear? She's going out. She's got her blue dress on and her earrings. And we're going to wait up. No matter how late. And when she gets home we're going to make her a cup of tea and she's going to tell us what she did and about all the people she met and how she danced and how she just had the best time ever. Hey, Orton?

> *Pause…* ORTON *doesn't answer.*

I'm cold.

> ORTON *scrummages for clothing and lays it out over* STACEY—*old coats and dresses—until she's just a tiny figure under a bundle of clothes. Then he lays down beside her and puts his arm around her.*

ORTON: You warm now?

STACEY: Yeah.

ORTON: Are you still bleeding?

STACEY: A bit. [*Pause.*] Can we go home, Orton? In the morning, can we go home?

ORTON: Yeah… Sssh now. Go to sleep… What's our brother's name?

STACEY: Mickey.

ORTON: Don't forget now.

STACEY: I won't.

> *The lights fade… until just the candle is burning.* RHONDA *begins her story.*

◆ ◆ ◆ ◆ ◆

TRASH

RHONDA MONOLOGUE

Carol says, 'Problem with you, Rhonda, problem with you is that you're just too fertile. You just got to look at a man and you're up the duff.' And we laughed but she's right, she's fucking right. Woman from
Welfare says, 'It must be hard. Must be hard for you, Rhonda, with all
those kids. Looking after them, it must be hard.' And I say, 'No. It's not hard.' Though it is. I know it and she knows it. But I'm not going to give her the satisfaction. So I say, 'No. Those kids, those kids are my blessings. Everyone of them a blessing. You understand. A blessing.'
Though it is… hard. But it's like Carol says I only got to look at a man.

Anyway, I'm down the pub playing the bandits when Carol, she's my neighbour, lives in the flat next door, Carol comes in and says, 'Cops were over your place earlier', and I said, 'Oh yeah, what do they want this time? If it's Nathan, you can tell 'em he's not there. Tell 'em he's pissed off.' Without a word mind you and with the rent. Bastard. And I'm not taking him back, not this time. No fucking way. Better off alone.

Well, that's what Carol says. But she doesn't get it. I don't know how she does it. No man in her life. Two kids and no man, not even now and then. Still, that's her. Carol doesn't get it, Family Services don't get it, but it's how I am. It's my life and I like having a man around. So I've had a few. They don't stick around. Anyway, Carol says it's not Nathan they're after, it's about your kids.

What about my kids?

Orton, he's sharp as a tack and good-looking too, drop-dead gorgeous, they all say it, everyone, they all say it, I was that proud of him. Like his dad, drop-dead gorgeous. Bastard though. His dad. Didn't stick around longer than he had to. But he'll get by, Orton, he's smart. Should be back at school. They all say it, all his teachers. 'Make him finish school', they say, and I say, 'You fuckin' make him finish school, you're his teachers'. What am I meant to do?

Anyway, Nathan's giving him a hard time so he pisses off. Well, he'd done it before, he'd take off, be back in a couple of days. I stopped asking questions 'cause he never tells me. It's his life, he doesn't have to tell me everything. But this time Nathan was giving it to him hard, hitting him hard and so I told him, Orton, I told him, get out, get out before the bastard kills you. It was for his own good. I did it for him.

Now Stace, my Stace, she's another matter. No matter how much school she does it's not going to make a difference. Better off at home, I reckon, keeping out of trouble. 'Cause she's not all there but I love her all the same. Something went wrong with Stace. I know it. Orton knows it too. We never say anything but we both know it. Stace isn't all there. Bless her and she loves her mum and her brother. She loves Orton, thinks he's the greatest in the world.

Couldn't stand it when he took off. Couldn't sleep, wet the bed at night. I was that riled with her with the bed wetting, night after night, could have slapped her but I never touched her, not Stace, never. Given Orton plenty but Orton can take it, but not Stace.

Anyway, it gets to a point when I can't stand it any longer, 'When's Orton coming home, Mum? When's Orton coming back?' So I tell her, 'You go and find him, go on, you go and find him and tell him to come home'.

Well, I didn't think she'd do it, but off she went stubborn as you like and I had to chase her, give her some money and a coat in case she had to stay out that night 'cause I knew she wouldn't come back without him, not once she'd got the idea into her head, so I knew she'd need something. Anyway, Nathan had turned up the night before so it was for the best. I did it for her really, told her to go and find Orton. I knew Orton would take care of her while I sorted out the thing with Nathan. So it was for the best.

And Mickey. Well Welfare's got Mickey. And they're not giving him back, not now.

And so anyway, Carol comes down to the pub and says they want to see you about your kids. And so I know there's trouble. Stacey's probably been picked up shoplifting or something. Doesn't bother me 'cause I taught 'em how. So I go down to the station and they know me there. And I say, 'Where are they? I want to see my kids.' But they keep me waiting while they make some calls and who they're calling I wouldn't know. I mean they don't tell me nothing. They don't say nothing.

Until they tell me to get in the car and they drive me down here. To this place. And this bloke comes out, this bloke in a suit comes out and says, 'You can't smoke in here'. And I say, 'Have you got my kids? Are my kids here?' And he looks all confused and says, 'Yes', and I say, 'Good, then I want to see them'. But he says, 'You can't see them', and I look at him and I say, 'I'm their mother and I can see them whenever I bloody well like'. And then he says it. Just a couple of words, he says it: 'There's been an accident'.

Pause.

'What accident?'

'A fire. There's been a fire. In a Brotherhood bin. A candle. The clothes. I'm sorry.'

Pause.

I want to see them and they say they advise against it and I say I don't care what you advise, I want to see my kids so they show me in.

And there they are, my Orton and Stace, all black from the fire and burnt together like one. But I can tell, I can see him. That's Orton, he's lying with his arm 'round Stace. Holding her. Like I knew he would. And he says, the man in the suit, he says, 'They didn't suffer, the smoke, it would have…'

She holds up her hand as if to motion him to stop talking.

And I say, 'They suffered. You don't know how much.'

And then someone says we can separate them for burial and I say no…

You won't touch 'em. That's how they died. You leave 'em that way. They're my blessings and you're not to touch 'em.

❖ ❖ ❖ ❖ ❖

DREAM-TOWN

SCENE FOUR

A police station.

The two GIRLS *are just in their evening dresses. The two school uniforms etc, are hanging up on the wall like little people. They are talking to another* POLICEMAN.

KATINA: Can we go now?

COP TWO: 'Fraid not.

KATINA: Can't you just charge us with shoplifting and let us go?

COP TWO: It's a bit more serious than shoplifting now, isn't it?

KATINA: What do you mean?

COP TWO: Impersonation. That's a crime.

KATINA: Us putting on school uniforms is a crime…

COP TWO: If you don't go to that school it is… and you two wouldn't have a chance in hell of going there, would ya…?

TRISHA: We're doing fine thanks very much.

COP TWO: Not right at the moment you're not.

KATINA: This is crap you know. It's crap. You can't go to jail for dressing up.

COP TWO: That's one word for it. I can think of other words for it. Deception, fraud, trickery, impersonation. All in the same criminal family…

TRISHA: We didn't trick anybody.

COP TWO: You shouldn't have had those uniforms on. You're not allowed to dress up in other people's clothes.

KATINA: Since when?

COP TWO: Since always. It's the law. You're not allowed to dress up like a policeman unless you're a policeman. You're not allowed to dress up like a fireman unless you're a fireman. It's dangerous and confusing. That's what clothes are for, so you can tell everyone apart from everyone else. Life isn't one big fancy-dress party. Life is for real. Everyone should look like what they are, or society will irretrievably breakdown…

KATINA: You're crazy, man.

COP TWO: In my opinion the law doesn't go far enough. In my opinion men shouldn't dress like women. Women shouldn't dress like men. Children shouldn't dress like adults and adults shouldn't dress like children. People shouldn't dress like animals. Animals shouldn't dress like people. It's un-Australian. We're an honest sort of country. Up-front. Wouldn't you say?

The GIRLS *aren't particularly interested.*

Now what I'd really like to know is where the real owners of these uniforms are…

The GIRLS *giggle.*

And what are they wearing?

The GIRLS *giggle.*

Where did you get the uniforms?

TRISHA: … Found 'em.

COP TWO: Did ya?

KATINA: Yeah we found them.

COP TWO: Where d'ja find 'em?

After a pause…

KATINA: In a Brotherhood bin.

COP TWO: In a Brotherhood bin?

KATINA: Yeah. In a Brotherhood bin.

The COP *seems to lose some of his casual attitude.*

COP TWO: You homeless, are you?

KATINA: Nah…

COP TWO: You better be careful what you're saying… both of you.

KATINA: We aren't homeless.

COP TWO: Why won't you tell me your names and addresses?

KATINA: Maybe we will.

She looks at TRISHA.

COP TWO: What were you doing inside a Brotherhood bin?

KATINA: They weren't inside the bin. They were sitting next to it folded up in a box.

COP TWO: What were they doing there?

KATINA: I dunno.

COP TWO: They look in very good condition. Why would someone leave them next to a Brotherhood bin?

KATINA: I dunno, do I? They were just there. Some girl probably finished school, or left school, or moved to another school, I dunno. Maybe she died, I dunno.

COP TWO: Who?

KATINA: I don't know who. I don't know her.

COP TWO: Where is this Brotherhood bin?

KATINA: Can't remember... they all look alike don't they? Can we go now?

COP TWO: How'd the blood get on the sleeve?

TRISHA: Someone pricked me with a pin.

COP TWO: Are you a junkie?

TRISHA: No.

COP TWO: Give me your arm.

They tussle.

TRISHA: No fuck off... fuck off.

KATINA: What are we meant to have done?

COP TWO: You tell me...

KATINA: Look we found them next to a Brotherhood bin. The hats and everything. I don't know whose they were.

COP TWO: What did they look like?

BOTH: Who?

COP TWO: The girls that wore these uniforms.

TRISHA: There aren't any girls. They don't exist.

COP TWO: They must exist. These are their uniforms.

KATINA: If they did they'd be identical twins, wouldn't they? Big fat identical twins. I don't think so.

COP TWO: Twins. Where did you meet them?

KATINA: We never met them. They don't go to our school. We don't know them.

COP TWO: But you've watched them?

KATINA: We never watched anybody.

COP TWO: What school do you go to?

The GIRLS *don't reply.*

Do you know who you remind me of? Those two girls in New Zealand, lived in their own little dream-town, lesbians more than likely, took one of their mothers for a walk and killed her with a brick. Do you know that story?

The two GIRLS *stare at him in silence.*

Are you lesbians?

They say nothing.

Just wondered… I saw you on film. Putting lipstick on each other's mouths.

KATINA: That's none of your business. I want to go home now. My name is Katina Nizamis. My phone number is 97638745.

He writes this down.

COP TWO: Ahuh… and your address?

KATINA: 19 Kelly Street Coburg.

COP TWO: Thanks, Katina. [*He looks at* TRISHA.] Do you want to go home?

TRISHA: Nuh.

COP TWO: Come on what's your name?

TRISHA: … Trisha.

COP TWO: Trisha what?

TRISHA: Trisha Falconetti. We don't have a phone.

COP TWO: Address?

TRISHA: Flat 26, 11 Hover Road, North Coburg.

The COP *finishes writing and stares into the air for a long moment.*

KATINA: Can we go now please?

He gets up and walks out from behind the desk. He is wearing an amazing pair of Nikes. The GIRLS *both stare in amazement at the shoes as he walks over to a shelf and picks up a book.*

I'm going to show you a book full of facial features and I want you to identify those similar to what those girls looked like.

He walks back and sits down behind the desk.

TRISHA: There aren't any girls. It's bullshit you know. We didn't find those uniforms in a Brotherhood bin. They're my mother's. She makes school uniforms, you know, for a living. So I don't know what the big deal is about this Brotherhood bin, but there wasn't any Brotherhood bin and there wasn't any girls and we have told you our names and addresses you know and you have to contact our parents or our legal guardian and we have to be let go, we are fifteen, you have to let us go.

COP TWO: Just take a look at the book.

TRISHA: Look you saw yourself. They're like new. That's 'cause they are new. No one has ever worn them except us. Why don't you send someone 'round? She'll be at home. She's always at home. It's all she ever does, sits at home and sews those stupid fucking uniforms.

COP TWO: Don't swear.

TRISHA: Don't swear? We've been here for hours. We've been here for days…

KATINA: Are you allowed to wear them to work?

COP TWO: What?

KATINA: Those Nikes.

COP TWO: What are Nikes?

KATINA: You know. Nikes… Nikes. Everyone knows what Nikes are.

He looks at her blankly.

Your shoes, are you allowed to wear those shoes?

COP TWO: I'm allowed to wear shoes. Isn't everybody?

KATINA: Where did you get them?

COP TWO: Where did I get my shoes?

KATINA: Yeah, where did you get them?

COP TWO: They're standard issue.

KATINA: Oh sure, like every cop's walking around with mad new Nikes on. I know everyone kills Nikes but I myself haven't seen cops wearing them.

COP TWO: I dunno what you're talking about.

He puts his feet up on the desk. He has normal police-issue, black, shiny shoes on. The GIRLS *stare at them.*

KATINA: We know about the body. We know about it. So there's no use pretending, there's no use trying to scare us.

TRISHA: Katina.

COP TWO: What do you know about it?

KATINA: We know there wasn't a mark on it. We know about you and your shoes. We know about The Keepers. It's this whole cover-up. 'Cause you've found an alien, or an alien escaped, anyway there's this dead alien, you know, floating down the river and you are wearing its shoes. I hope they infect you, man, I hope they give you some crazy virus unknown on earth and your body gets covered in pusy sores and you melt away. You shouldn't steal shoes off dead aliens, especially not if you're a cop.

COP TWO: I don't know what you're talking about.

KATINA: You know what I'm talking about, you know what I'm talking about.

COP TWO: Nope.

KATINA: The body in the river.

COP TWO: There wasn't a body in the river.

KATINA: You're a fucking liar!

COP TWO: If you're talking about this so-called unidentified body, it wasn't found in the river.

TRISHA: I told you, Katina.

KATINA: I saw it on television.

TRISHA: It was the city square, wasn't it? It was wedged under the statue of Burke and Wills.

COP TWO: It wasn't wedged under Burke and Wills. It wasn't tied to the water wall and it didn't come out a chute from the toilets in the casino and go floating down the Yarra. It's all crap. It's all fantasy. It was in a Brotherhood bin, or to be precise, they were in a Brotherhood bin. There were two bodies. Two strange small bodies, so disfigured that even the experts can't tell what they are. They were tied together, holding each other, like something out of Pompeii, do you know what that is?

TRISHA: What do you think? We killed someone. Is that what you think? You're sick. I wouldn't hurt a fly. I'm fucking vegetarian. Why would I kill anybody?

COP TWO: You haven't got much, have you?

TRISHA: What do you mean, money, you mean?

COP TWO: Don't you get envious?

TRISHA: Nah.

COP TWO: Don't you get angry?

TRISHA: Nah.

COP TWO: When you see the girls that have got everything?

TRISHA: Nah.

COP TWO: What are you going to do with your life?

TRISHA: Haven't made my mind up yet.

KATINA: Not going to be a cop, that's for sure.

COP TWO: You've got nothing.

TRISHA: We haven't got nothing.

COP TWO: You've got nothing.

TRISHA: We haven't got nothing. We haven't got nothing. We're fucking smart. We know how things operate. We see the inside of things, the messy bitching ugly inside of things, not just the nice things, not just the prettied-up fucking bits. We're fucking smart, so don't you tell us we've got nothing, you fucking prick! We haven't got nothing. Have we, Katina? We haven't got nothing!

◆ ◆ ◆ ◆ ◆

SUIT

SCENE THREE

The stage is bare except for a Brotherhood bin. Besides it sits GINA DE STANZO, *dressed in black, at her feet a bunch of flowers.* JAMIE *passes by. He stops. From his pocket he pulls out a coin. He throws it at* GINA.

Note: GINA *will speak in her native language throughout the dialogue (Italian or Greek, depending on the actor).*

GINA: *Child, no, no. I'm not begging. I'm just grieving.*

JAMIE: My apologies.

GINA: *That's all right. I begged once, as a child, I've promised myself I'd never do it again.*

JAMIE: Why are you grieving?

GINA: *My son is dead.*

JAMIE: I'm sorry. Why are you sitting here?

GINA: *It's here where they found him.*

JAMIE: How did he die?

GINA: *They don't know. They won't tell me anything. They refuse to show me the body.*

JAMIE: Are you sure it's your son?

GINA: *Yes. God told me.*

> JAMIE *is silent.*

You don't believe me.

JAMIE: No.

GINA: *He told me. In a dream. He showed me this place.*

JAMIE: How old was your son?

GINA: *Sixteen.*

JAMIE: Did he run away?

> GINA *is silent.*

How long has he been missing?

GINA: *A year.*

JAMIE: Maybe he's still alive.

GINA: *No. God does not lie.*

JAMIE: Yes he does. He promised that the deluge would not come again. But then, what's this? [*He sits, pointing across the stage.*] This world, your loss, isn't this all another deluge?

GINA: *God did not lie. He promised the fire next time.* [*She points around the stage.*] *This is the fire.*

JAMIE: How long have you been here?

GINA: *Days.*

JAMIE: Are you married?

GINA: *My husband has to work. He doesn't believe that God spoke to me, he doesn't believe in God. My husband believes in work. He works very hard and he believes in it. He and my son used to argue all the time about work. Sammy thought our son lazy. We De Stanzos are workers, he used to say. We should be proud of that. He called my son a bludger. My son didn't believe in work.*

JAMIE: And do you believe in work?

GINA: *No. That's very strange. No one has ever asked me that question. No, I don't believe in work.*

JAMIE: It's very cold. Isn't your husband worried?

GINA: *He thinks I'm mad.*

JAMIE: Are you?

GINA: *No.*

JAMIE: I think I am. I think I'm mad.

GINA: *No. You're not mad either. You're young.*

JAMIE: And black.

GINA *stares at him, then nods.*

GINA: *Yes, you're black.*

JAMIE: Why did your son leave?

GINA: *I don't know.*

JAMIE: I left home, at fifteen.

GINA: *Why did you leave?*

JAMIE: I had to. Or I thought I had to. Or maybe I wanted to and I didn't really have to. I don't know either anymore. Why did you leave home?

GINA: *Because it was tough at home and there was a place to go.*

JAMIE: So did you have to leave or did you want to leave?

GINA: *Both. Sometimes it can be both.*

JAMIE: So you came here.

GINA: *In those matters there was no choice. When you're poor there are only a few places where you can go. I was accepted here.*

JAMIE: And where were you from?

GINA: *Greece/Italy.*

JAMIE: I'd like to go there.

GINA: *Yes, you'd like it. Do you work?*

JAMIE: I'm retrenched. This week. No, I guess I don't work.

GINA: *I'm sorry. It's tough, isn't it? My husband complains a lot, he thinks Australians are bludgers, but jobs are hard to get. I know.*

JAMIE: I'll get a job.

GINA: *Good. My son was unemployed.*

JAMIE: I will get a job. I'm going to try really hard.

GINA: *My son was young, fifteen, he didn't want to work. We complained too much. We wanted him back at school. We were too harsh.*

JAMIE: I've done a course, in computers. I'm qualified, I'm not stupid, eh? And I'm not lazy. And I don't drink.

GINA: *My son drank all the time. And he took drugs. That worries me. Maybe that's how he died.*

JAMIE: I told you, I don't drink!

GINA: *Why aren't you listening to me?!*

JAMIE: [*at the same time*] Why aren't you listening to me?!

> *Silence.* JAMIE *stands up and opens his briefcase. He begins to throw the books and magazines into the bin.*

GINA: *That's good. Books are good, they take your mind off things. I never throw old books away, I give them away.*

JAMIE: What are your favourite books?

GINA: *The fairytales, it's always been the fairytales. And I read* The Thorn Birds. *That was good.*

JAMIE: Have you read the Bible?

GINA: *Some. Some of it is too difficult.*

JAMIE: So how do you know God? Because He speaks to you?

GINA: *No. He's never spoken before. I've always believed in God.*

JAMIE: Always, you've never doubted once?

GINA: *No, not once.*

JAMIE: Never?

GINA: *No. Never.*

JAMIE: Even when your son was gone?

> *Silence.* JAMIE *throws the last book into the chute. It is the Communist Manifesto.*

Once you've begun to doubt you can never go back, can you?

GINA: *Yes you can.*

JAMIE: How?

GINA: *By prayer.*

JAMIE: Not action.

GINA: *I'm talking about God, my friend. Prayer is the only action he requires.*

JAMIE: Will your son know God?

GINA: *Yes.*

JAMIE: Did he believe? Did your son believe?

Silence.

So he won't know God.

GINA: *Stop. My son will know God!*

JAMIE: Did he believe?

GINA: *Please, stop.*

JAMIE: Just this question. Did he believe?

GINA: [*softly*] *No.*

JAMIE: Then he's like me.

GINA: *You make God sound so cruel.*

JAMIE: He is nothing. He isn't there.

GINA: *He is, for all of us. He listens to everyone of us.*

JAMIE: Your God, He's kind, isn't he?

GINA: [*beginning to smile*] *Yes.*

JAMIE: Your God is compassionate.

GINA: [*her eyes closed, in prayer*] *Yes.*

JAMIE: Your God protects you.

GINA: [*ecstatically*] *Yes.*

JAMIE: Your God will save you.

GINA: *Yes, yes.*

JAMIE: Your God is white.

GINA: *Yes.*

Silence. She stops. Her eyes open, her face falls to sadness.

Yes, I'm sorry. I should have lied. I'm sorry, in my heart God is white.

JAMIE: No, I'm glad. I know God is white. [*He stands up and puts out his hand.*] Let me take you home. It's getting dark and it's cold.

GINA: *I can't leave. Not till God tells me to. Not till I can bury my son.*

JAMIE: Can I at least buy you something to eat?

GINA: *No, save your money. You'll need it. Thank you, I'll be fine.*

JAMIE: This won't bring him back. If he's dead, this won't bring back your son.

GINA: *No. This won't bring him back.*

JAMIE leans over and kisses her. Their mouths touch to a short, wet kiss. She carefully touches his face. JAMIE is the first to pull apart. He takes off his jacket and puts it over the woman's shoulders. He exits the stage.

GINA is alone, she begins a soft prayer. We hear a radio.

NEWSREADER: And this afternoon the Federal Government announced that the first trial of its work-for-the-dole scheme has been a great success, with the

Victorian Chamber of Commerce releasing figures indicating many of its members would be happy to participate in the next stage of trials.

The identity of the body discovered in Dandenong on Friday is still baffling police. Watch *A Current Affair* tonight for a special report on the mystery.

In the Middle East a bomb detonated in a busy Jerusalem market killing seven Israelis and eight Palestinians. The radical Muslim group HAMAS is suspected of being behind the atrocity.

And in sports news, Sydney full forward Tony Lockett may miss a further two games due to an aggravated groin…

Slowly the prayers overpower the sound of the radio, of the street. A white light appears. The prayer and the light get stronger. GINA *strips and walks towards the light. It flashes blindingly intense for a moment. She has disappeared, ascended.*

The prayers and the light have gone. On the empty stage: her flowers, her dress, JAMIE'*s jacket.*

❖ ❖ ❖ ❖ ❖

MONEY

SCENE FOUR: COMFORT MONOLOGUE

A bedroom. The WOMAN *sits up suddenly in the bed. She has just awoken. She quickly checks the time on her watch and then she relaxes. There is a sleeping* MAN *lying next to her. She gently leans over him and listens to his breathing.*

WOMAN: Sleep. Sleep.

She touches his face. She gets up, careful not to disturb the sleeping MAN.

He fell at my feet. Never had a man fall at my feet before. He literally fell, at my feet, in the street. In Sydney Road. Of all the people he could have fallen in front of, he chose me. And I thought: Fuck! Why me?! I tried to get other people to help but not on your life, they weren't going to have a bar of him or me. Probably thought he was drunk. I did. I said, get up, you silly bugger, get up. But he was sick, not drunk, sick and he asked me to call him a taxi and by the time one of them took notice of me and pulled over, he was up on his feet but real groggy and looking drunker than drunk and the taxi driver was shaking his head and the only way I could get him to take him was if I got in too. So I took him home and he only lives two streets away from me so it wasn't any big deal. I helped him inside and on to this bed. And then I said, I've got to go. Will you be all right? I've got to go. I wanted to get out of there before he got more sick or he died or something. Then he opened his eyes, his beautiful eyes and he thanked me. He got out his wallet and I said, don't be silly. I don't want your money. You gave me a lift. I only live two streets away. But he insisted and he took out two hundred dollars and held it out to me. I couldn't believe my eyes. Two hundred dollars! You've got to be kidding. Is this bloke an easy take or what? I said, no, I couldn't. Two hundred dollars, on a silver platter being offered to me. It was like a miracle. That's all I needed. Two hundred dollars. I was short two hundred dollars. With that two hundred dollars I could pay that month's mortgage. It was kind of like it was meant to be. No, I couldn't, I said. And I took it. And I paid the mortgage. But I didn't feel good. I could barely eat or sleep. What's it matter, I thought. He offered it to me. I did him a good turn. I came back to tell him that I was so sorry I took his money. His door was open and I found him here where I'd last seen him. Asleep. And I thought what's sorry going to do, so I cleaned his house and I washed his clothes and I cooked him something to eat. When he woke he smiled when he saw me and went back to sleep. I came back the next day and the day after that. I've been coming for almost a year. No one knows I come. Only him and me know. When the district nurse comes I hide out the back until she's gone. One day she came early and I was in bed and I pulled the sheet over my head and lay as still as death and listened to her prattle on about it being time for him to give it up and come into hospital. He got the giggles and she asked him what he found so funny and checked to see if he was getting too much morph. On good days we sit and talk. He asks me about me. What about me, I say. Anything, he says. And so I tell him anything, anything that comes into my mind. Sometimes I fall asleep too. He's in my arms and it's so lovely and warm, I feel myself go. It's irresistible. I think I sleep more sound here than in my own bed at home. Some days there's no talk and no sleep. Painful days. Now he's smaller I cup him into me and I whisper, sh, sh, sh, shush now, shush now, and I think I'm holding my baby. My sweet little boy. My Daniel. How long since I held you? And then I think, who's got the pain here, me or you? Sometimes when I hold him and at last he gets some relief and sleeps, I lie there and I imagine I'm having an affair. And we've just made passionate love. If I could I would make love to him. If his body wasn't quite so tired. When his body touches mine, the warmth of him, and his breathing, gentle as it is, is enough. I come. I do. You smell nice, he says to me, when he wakes sometimes. And I laugh. He pays me. I should be paying you, I think when I pocket it. He pays me for the cleaning, the cooking, for the company. I can't tell anyone that I come here. I can't. What could I say? I've got a job. What do you do, they'd ask. I couldn't explain it. I don't like to call it a job, it doesn't feel like a job. I like to get the money but I think he'd give it to me anyway.

MAN: Are you going?

WOMAN: No. Not yet.

She lifts the blankets and crawls into the bed next to him.

THE END

MUSIC CUES

These music cues are from the original production. Some scenes have since
  been reordered for this published version.

1 'Money'

   Played towards the end of *Kennett Monologue* and transition into *Money*.
   Cue: 'I can't wait to vote' (pg.3)

2 'Requiem 2' – march

   Played as a brisk march towards the end of *Money*. Cue: Daniel says '… I
   didn't take it, I swear. I didn't take it!' (pg.9)

3 'Money'

   Played towards the end of *Suit 1*. Cue: Claire spits on the notes (pg.15)

4 'Dream-Town 1'

   Played during transition from *Trash* into *Dream-Town*. Cue: Stacey calls
   out 'Orton' (pg.27)

5 'Dream-Town 2'

   Played directly after *Dream-Town 1*… fades out (pg.27)

6 'Dream-Town 2' – rap

   Played during transition from *Suit 2* into *Dream-Town 2*. Cue: When Trisha
   and Katina step onto the platform (pg.28)

7 'Requiem for the Working Class'

   Played towards the end of *Trash 2*. Cue: Orton shouts 'Fuck off'… fades
   out in *Train* (pg.32)

8 'Requiem for the Working Class'

   Underscores *Trash 3*. Cue: end of *Train* (pg.37)

9 'Money'

   Played during transition after *Leon Monolgue* going into *Break-In*. Cue: '…
   philosophers' (pg.41)

10 'Dream-Town 2'

   Transition from *Break-in* into *Dream-Town 3* (pg.46)

11 'Requiem for the Working Class' – fade out and fade in

   Played after *Dream-Town 3* going into *Trash 4*. When the scene is set (pg.48), fade out... when Orton and Stacey look into the candle (pg.51), resume playing from where you finished and play directly through to the end of 'Requiem 2' slowly (not a brisk march) and, if necessary, cycle back to 'Requiem for the Working Class'.

12 'Dream-Town 1'

Played directly after *Rhonda Monologue* finishes... going into *Dream-Town 4* (pg.55)

13 'Comfort'

Transition from *Dream-Town 4* into *Suit 3*. <u>Cue</u>: Trisha says 'We haven't got nothing'... fade out as soon as scene for *Suit 3* is set (pg.60)

14 'Comfort'

End of *Suit 3*... fade out when *Comfort Monologue* is set (pg.65)

15 'Comfort'

Play entire 'Comfort' theme under the remaining dialogue. <u>Cue</u>: Woman says 'He pays me' (pg.66)

MUSIC CONTENTS

MONEY

C Irine Vela 1998

REQUIEM
for the working class

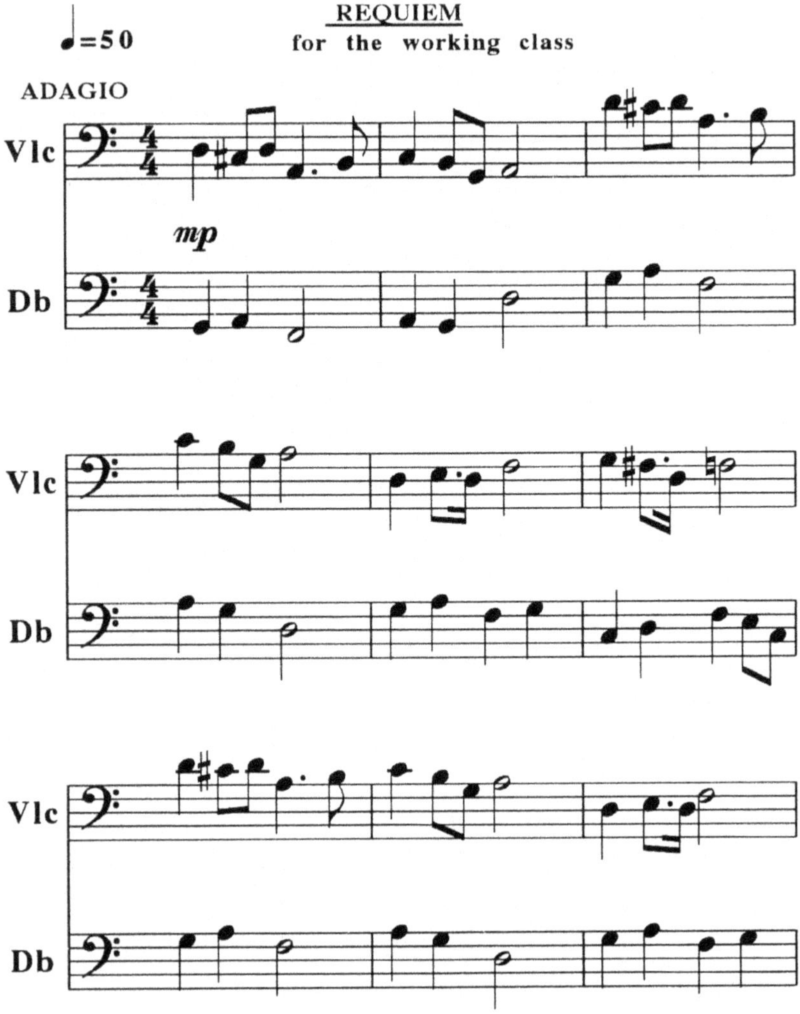

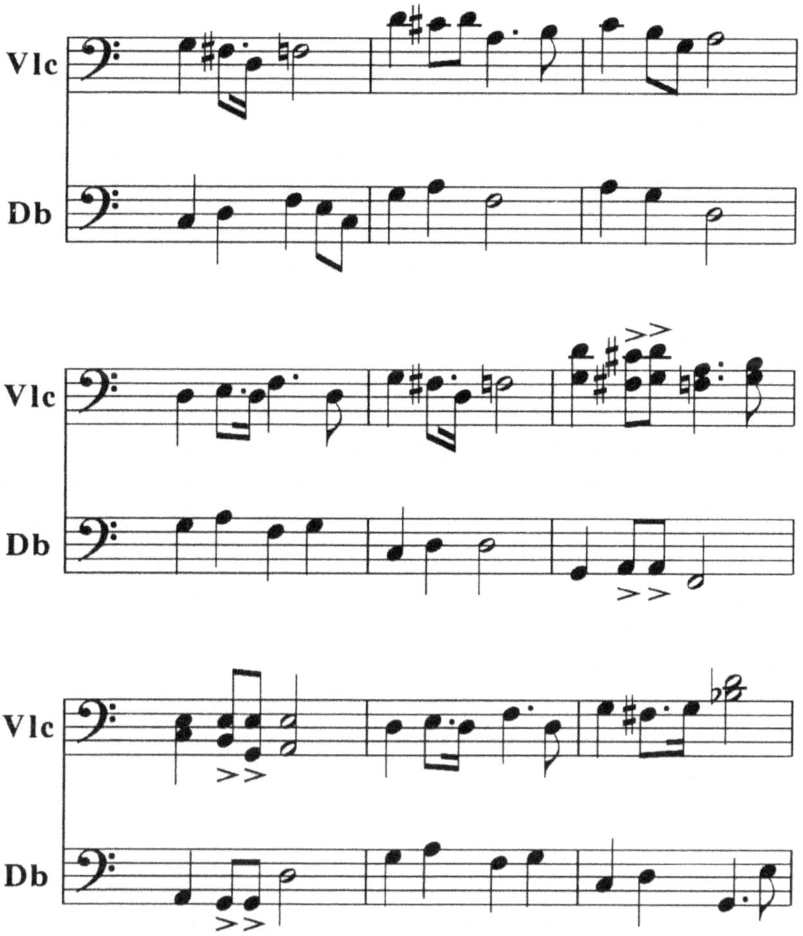
Vlc
Db
Vlc
Db
Vlc
Db

REQUIEM #2

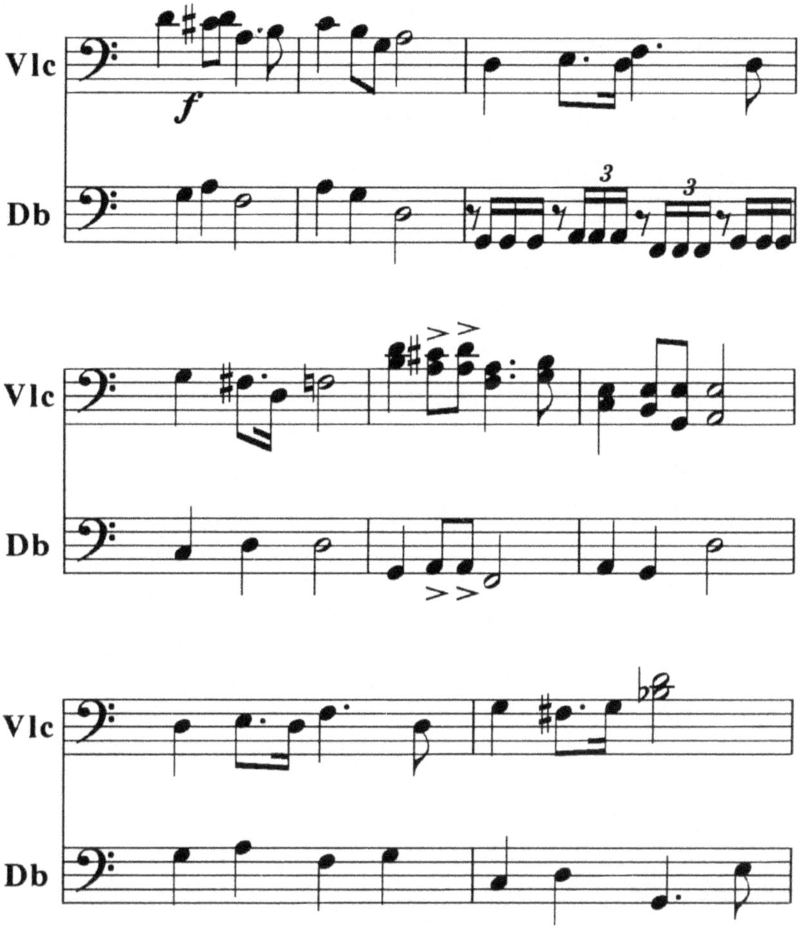
Vlc
Db
f
3
3
Vlc
Db
Vlc
Db

DREAMTOWN 1

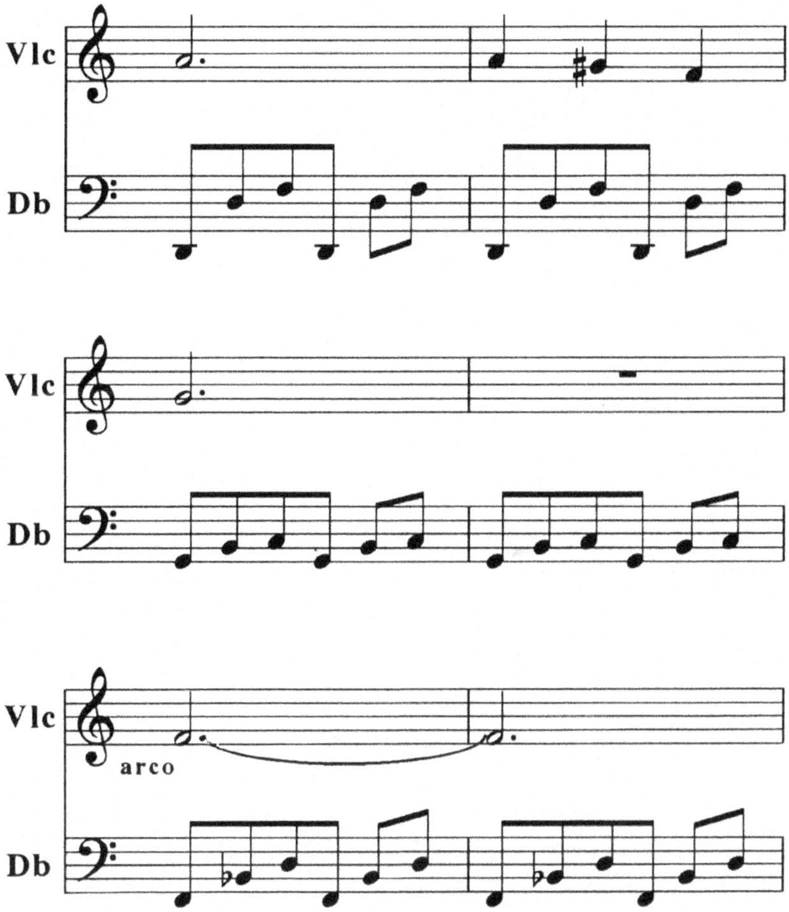
Vlc
Db
Vlc
Db
Vlc
arco
Db

c Irine Vela 1998

DREAM TOWN # 2

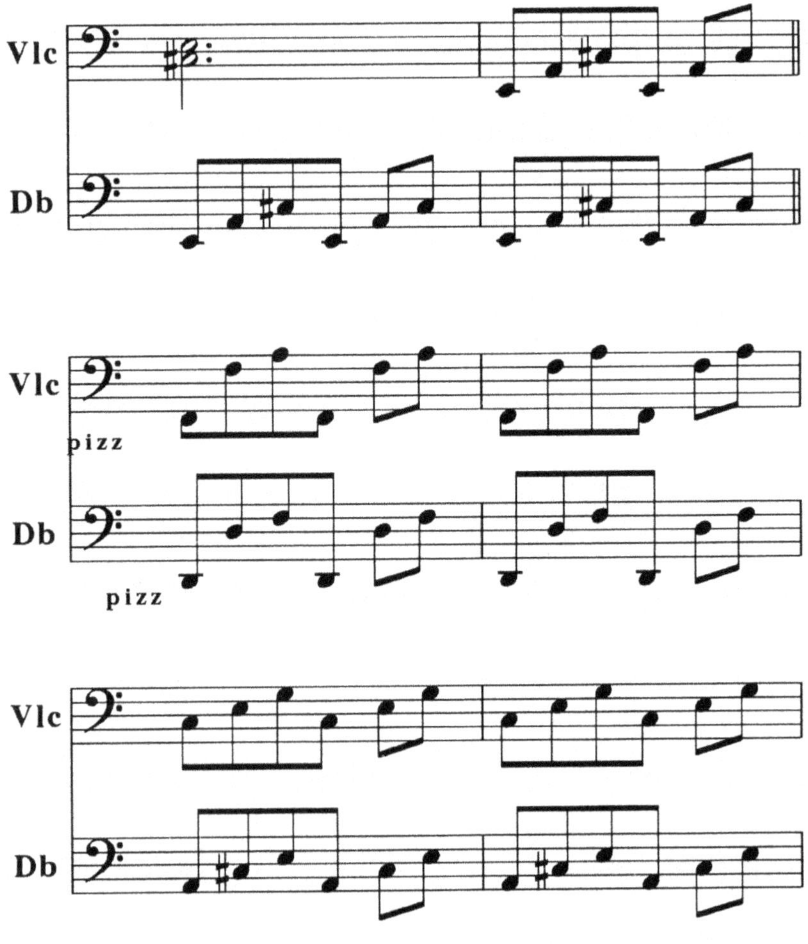
Vlc
Db
Vlc
pizz
Db
pizz
Vlc
Db

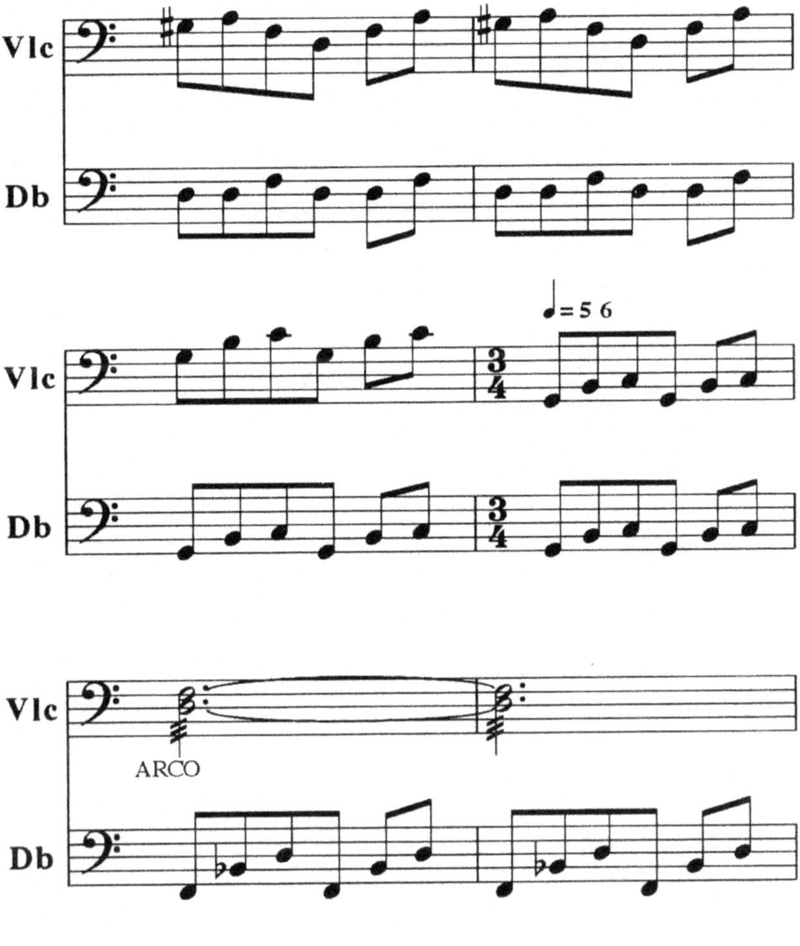
Vlc
Db
♩= 5 6
Vlc
Db
Vlc
ARCO
Db

COMFORT

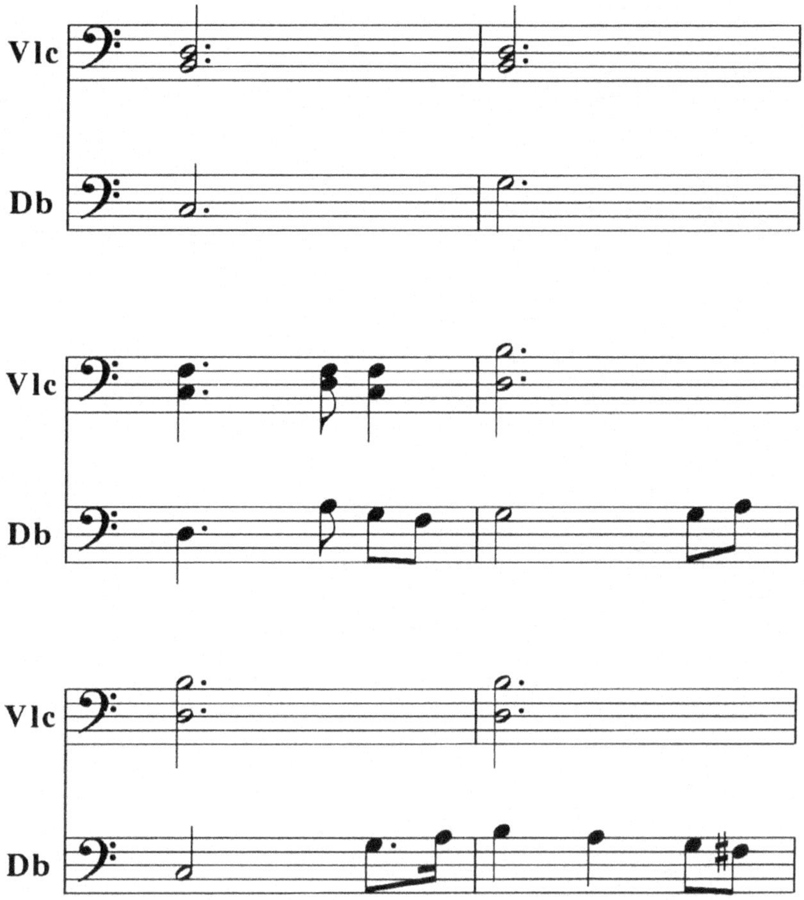
Vlc
Db
Vlc
Db
Vlc
Db

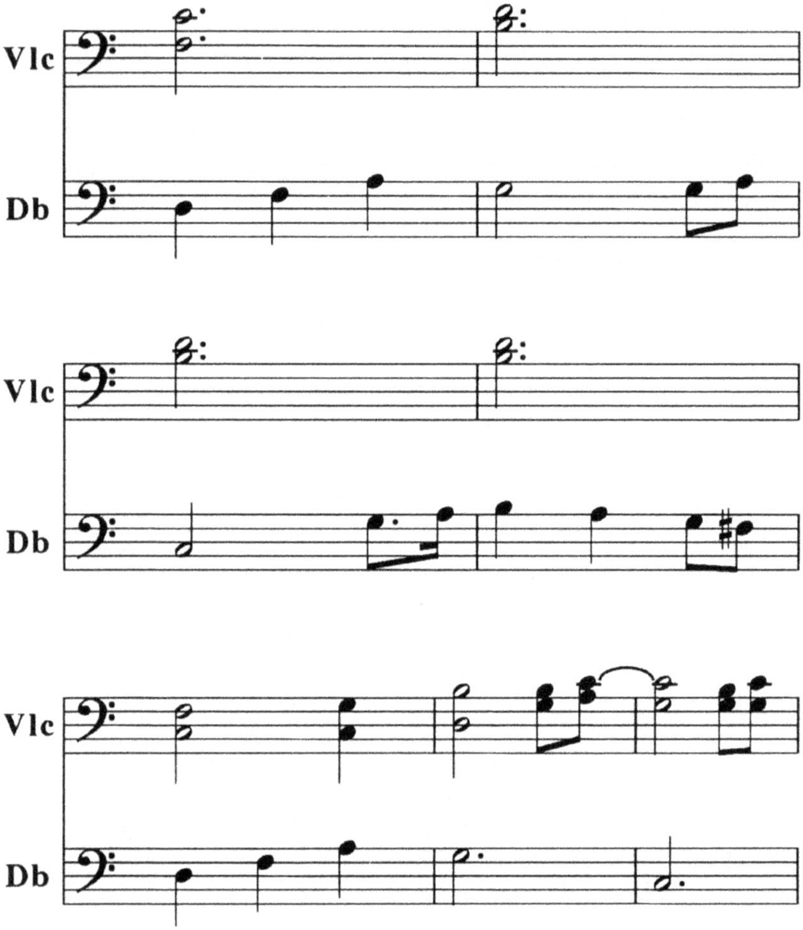
Vlc
Db
Vlc
Db
Vlc
Db

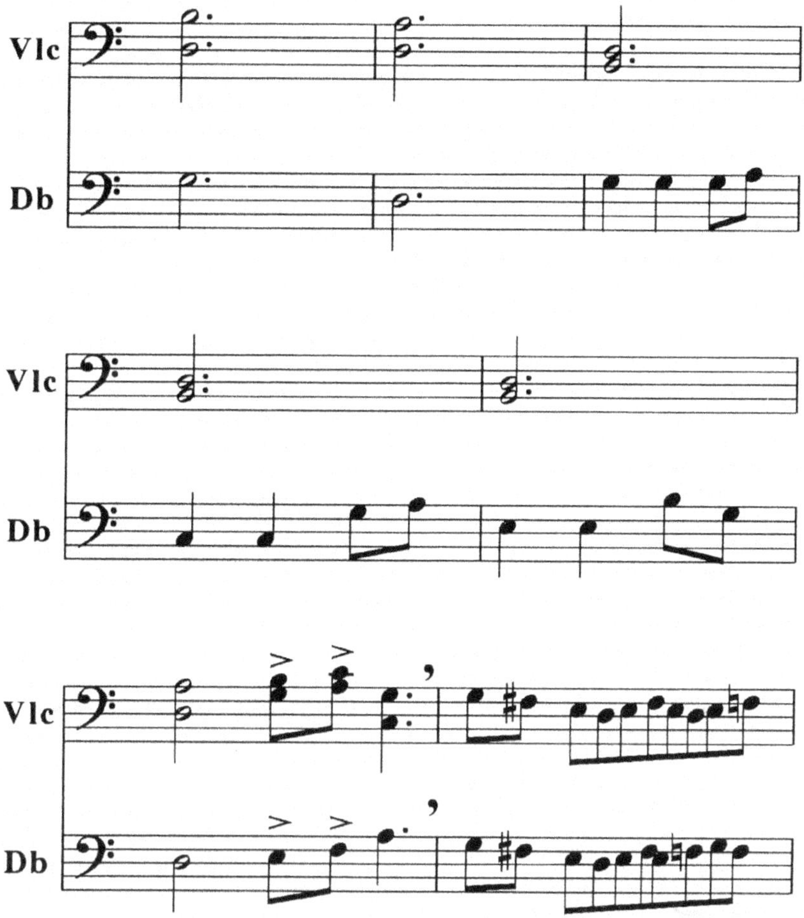
Vlc
Db
Vlc
Db
Vlc
Db

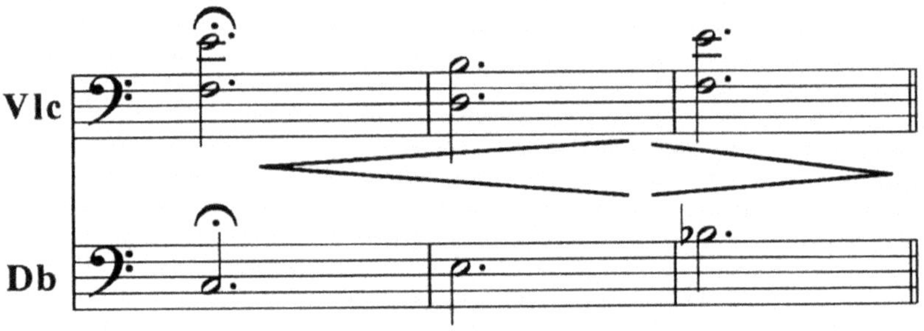
Vlc
Db

www.ingramcontent.com/pod-product-compliance
Lightning Source LLC
Chambersburg PA
CBHW050019090426
42734CB00021B/3329